Math Contests—Grades 7 and 8
Volume 2

School Years: 1982-83 through 1990-91

Steven R. Conrad ● Daniel Flegler

Published by MATH LEAGUE PRESS
Printed in the United States of America

Cover art by Bob DeRosa

Second Printing (revised), 1994

Copyright © 1992, 1994
by Mathematics Leagues Inc.
All Rights Reserved

Math League Press
P.O. Box 720
Tenafly, NJ 07670

ISBN 0-940805-05-7

Preface

The 2nd Math Contest Book for Grades 7 and 8 is the second volume in the series of problem books for students in these grades. The first volume contained the contests that were given from the 1977-78 school year through the 1981-82 school year. (A form you may use to order any of our books appears on page 166.) This volume contains the contests that were given from 1982-83 through 1990-91.

This book is divided into three sections for ease of use by both students and teachers. The first section of the book contains the contests. Each contest is a 40-question multiple-choice contest that can be worked in a 30-minute period. Each of the 3-page contests is designed so that questions on the 1st page are generally straightforward, those on the 2nd page are moderate in difficulty, and those on the 3rd page are more difficult. The second section of the book consists of detailed solutions to all the contest questions. The third and final section of the book consists of the letter answers to each contest and rating scales to evaluate individual performance.

Many people may prefer to consult the answer section rather than the solution section when first reviewing a contest. It is the experience of the authors that reworking a problem when the answer (but *not* the solution) is known frequently leads to increased understanding of problem-solving techniques.

Steven R. Conrad & Daniel Flegler, contest authors

Acknowledgments

For her continued patience and understanding, special thanks to Marina Conrad, whose only mathematical skill, an important one, is the ability to count the ways.

For her lifetime support and encouragement, special thanks to Mildred Flegler.

To Alan Feldman, who suggested several stylistic changes from the first volume to this one, we offer our thanks.

To Paul Ericksen and Mark Motyka, we offer our gratitude for their assistance over the years.

To Brian and Keith Conrad, who did an awesome proofreading job, thanks!

And the winning number...

Table Of Contents

1982-83 Annual 7th Grade Contest

Tuesday, February 8, 1983

7

Instructions

- **Time** You will have only *30 minutes* working time for this contest. You might be *unable* to finish all 40 questions in the time allowed.

- **Scores** Remember *this is a contest, not a test.* There is no "passing" or "failing" score. Few students score as high as 30 points (75% correct); students with even half that, 15 points, *deserve commendation!*

- **Format and Point Value** This is a multiple-choice contest. For each question, write the *capital letter* that is *in front of* the answer you choose. For each question, your answer will be one of the *capital letters* A, B, C, or D. Each question you answer correctly is worth 1 point. Unanswered questions receive no credit.

Copyright © 1983 by Mathematics Leagues Inc.

1

Answers

1. $1 - \frac{1}{1983} =$ A) 0 B) $\frac{1}{1983}$ C) $\frac{1981}{1982}$ D) $\frac{1982}{1983}$	1. D
2. $(4 - 3) \times (5 - 4) \times (6 - 5) \times (9 - 2) =$ A) 1 B) 7 C) 10 D) 21	2. B
3. $\sqrt{9} + \sqrt{16} =$ A) $\sqrt{5}$ B) $\sqrt{7}$ C) $\sqrt{25}$ D) $\sqrt{49}$	3. B
4. The total number of hours in the month of February, 1983 is A) 196 B) 696 C) 672 D) 720	4. C
5. 125% is the same as A) $\frac{4}{5}$ B) $\frac{5}{4}$ C) $\frac{6}{5}$ D) 125	5. B
6. Round off 43.846 to the nearest tenth. A) 40 B) 44 C) 43.8 D) 43.9	6. C
7. Find the missing number: $\frac{480}{44} = \frac{?}{11}$ A) 120 B) 132 C) 180 D) 1920	7. A
8. In every right triangle, two sides are always A) equal in length B) horizontal C) perpendicular D) vertical	8. C
9. $\frac{5}{10} \times \frac{6}{10} =$ A) 30 B) 3 C) 0.3 D) 0.03	9. C
10. If 3 times a number is 48, then one-fourth of the same number is A) 16 B) 4 C) 12 D) 30	10. B
11. $2^5 + 2^5 =$ A) 4^5 B) 4^{10} C) 4^{25} D) 2^6	11. D
12. The ratio of the sum of the angle measures of a triangle to the sum of the angle measures of a square is A) 1:2 B) 2:3 C) 3:4 D) 4:3	12. A
13. $0.25 + \frac{1}{2} =$ A) $\frac{2}{3}$ B) $\frac{3}{4}$ C) 1 D) $1\frac{1}{4}$	13. B
14. $0.8\overline{)17.624}$ A) 22.3 B) 2.203 C) 2.23 D) 22.03	14. D
15. The smallest one-digit prime is multiplied by the smallest two-digit prime. The product is A) 18 B) 22 C) 26 D) 33	15. B

Go on to the next page ⫸ **7**

2

Answers

---

16. Three-halves of one-half is

    A) $\frac{3}{4}$ B) $\frac{1}{4}$ C) $\frac{2}{3}$ D) $1\frac{1}{2}$

16. B

---

17. $(95 \times 68) - (94 \times 68) =$

    A) 1   B) 68   C) 78   D) 88

17. B

---

18. If a 3-digit whole number is multiplied by a 3-digit whole number, the product could have

    A) 3 digits   B) 5 digits   C) 7 digits   D) 9 digits

18. B

---

19. What number must be changed (in only *one* place) to make the horizontal and vertical totals all correct?

				total
9	3	2	2	16
8	2	7	1	20
2	1	4	3	10
6	8	3	5	22
total 25	14	16	13	8

    A) 1   B) 2   C) 3   D) 8

19. B

---

20. A man has 99¢ in change. If he has the fewest possible coins, how many nickels does he have?

    A) 0   B) 1   C) 2   D) 3

20. A

---

21. $\frac{2}{0.5} + \frac{5}{0.2} =$

    A) 29   B) $2\frac{1}{2}$ C) 1   D) $\frac{7}{10}$

21. A

---

22. $(5\frac{1}{3} - 2\frac{1}{2}) + (5\frac{1}{2} - 2\frac{1}{3}) =$

    A) 4   B) 5   C) 6   D) 7

22. C

---

23. Find the area of the rectangle if the radius of each circle is 4.

    A) 48   B) 96   C) 192   D) 384

23. D

---

24. 1.4 minutes =

    A) 64 seconds   B) 84 seconds   C) 96 seconds   D) 100 seconds

24. A

---

25. Event A occurs every 4 days, event B occurs every 6 days, and event C occurs every 8 days. If all three events occur on July 1, the next day that they will all occur together is

    A) July 9   B) July 19   C) July 24   D) July 25

25. D

---

26. If angle DAB and angle DBC are right angles, then $DC =$

    A) 5   B) 13   C) 17   D) 18

26. B

---

27. Three goats eat 6 tin cans in 1 hour. How long should it take six goats to eat 3 tin cans?

    A) 15 minutes   B) 30 minutes   C) 1 hour   D) 2 hours

27. B

---

28. Which is true?

    A) $\frac{1}{7} > \frac{1}{3}$ B) $\frac{2}{9} < \frac{1}{5}$ C) $\frac{2}{3} > \frac{7}{10}$ D) $\frac{5}{7} < \frac{8}{9}$

28. D

---

3   Go on to the next page ▶   **7**

29. 0.3% = A) $\frac{1}{3}$ B) $\frac{3}{10}$ C) $\frac{3}{100}$ D) $\frac{3}{1000}$	29. B
30. A girl began shopping with $15. After spending some money, the amount she had left was equal to $\frac{2}{3}$ of what she had spent. How much had she spent? A) $5 B) $6 C) $9 D) $10	30. A
31. The lengths of the sides of an isosceles triangle are 6 cm and 12 cm. The perimeter of the triangle is A) 18 cm B) 30 cm C) 36 cm D) 72 cm	31. B
32. A room is one-half full of people. After 20 people leave, the room is one-third full. When full, the room holds A) 60 people B) 80 people C) 90 people D) 120 people	32. A
33. 26^6 = A) 308 915 772 B) 308 915 774 C) 308 915 776 D) 308 915 778	33. C
34. If 14 *whosits* equals 35 *whatsits*, then 50 *whatsits* equals A) 125 *whosits* B) 70 *whosits* C) 20 *whosits* D) 7 *whosits*	34. C
35. Which of the following has a value different from the others? A) 15×28×33 B) 9×35×88 C) 12×77×15 D) 22×30×21	35. B
36. Find the missing number: $\frac{1}{8} + \frac{3}{8} = \frac{1}{7} + \frac{?}{7}$ A) 3 B) 4 C) $2\frac{1}{2}$ D) $3\frac{1}{2}$	36. D
37. A gear 48 cm in diameter turns a smaller gear 36 cm in diameter. In the time the larger gear makes 12 revolutions, how many revolutions does the smaller gear make? A) 24 B) 16 C) 12 D) 9	37. A
38. In the pattern of unit squares shown in the diagram, the shaded area is A) 2 sq. units B) 3 sq. units C) 5 sq. units D) 6 sq. units	38. B
39. The hundreds' digit of $\sqrt{999\,999}$ is A) 3 B) 5 C) 7 D) 9	39. D
40. A pilot flew 80 km. He flew the first 4 minutes at half speed and the second 4 minutes at full speed. The full speed of the plane is A) 400 km/hr B) 600 km/hr C) 800 km/hr D) 1000 km/hr	40. C

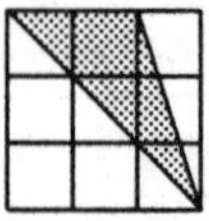

The end of the contest 🕮   **7**

Solutions on Page 73 • Answers on Page 146

1983-84 Annual 7th Grade Contest

Tuesday, February 14, 1984

7

Instructions

- **Time** You will have only *30 minutes* working time for this contest. You might be *unable* to finish all 40 questions in the time allowed.

- **Scores** Remember *this is a contest, not a test.* There is no "passing" or "failing" score. Few students score as high as 30 points (75% correct); students with even half that, 15 points, *deserve commendation!*

- **Format and Point Value** This is a multiple-choice contest. For each question, write the *capital letter* that is *in front of* the answer you choose. For each question, your answer will be one of the *capital letters* A, B, C, or D. Each question you answer correctly is worth 1 point. Unanswered questions receive no credit.

Answers

1. $1 \times 9 \times 8 \times 4 =$ A) 288 B) 289 C) 984 D) 1984	1. A
2. Which of the following is a quadrilateral? A) pentagon B) hexagon C) circle D) square	2. D
3. $333^2 =$ A) 666 B) 999 C) 110 889 D) 333 333	3. C
4. $4\frac{1}{4} - 2\frac{1}{2} =$ A) $2\frac{1}{2}$ B) $2\frac{3}{4}$ C) $1\frac{1}{4}$ D) $1\frac{3}{4}$	4. D
5. The largest prime factor of 7 000 000 is A) 7 B) 11 C) 13 D) 17	5. A
6. $0.5 + 0.55 + 0.555 =$ A) 0.605 B) 1.555 C) 1.605 D) 1.695	6. C
7. $(\frac{1}{2} + \frac{2}{3} + \frac{3}{4}) + (\frac{1}{2} + \frac{1}{3} + \frac{1}{4}) =$ A) 1 B) $2\frac{1}{12}$ C) $2\frac{11}{12}$ D) 3	7. D
8. Which is the greatest common divisor of 1983 and 1985? A) 0 B) 1 C) 3 D) 5	8. B
9. $0.02 \times 0.32 =$ A) 0.0064 B) 0.064 C) 0.64 D) 64	9. B
10. A right triangle *cannot* have an angle of measure A) 1° B) 89° C) 90° D) 91°	10. D
11. $\frac{1982}{1983} \div \frac{1982}{1984} =$ A) 1 B) $1\frac{1}{1983}$ C) $1\frac{1}{1984}$ D) 1984	11. B
12. The average of $\frac{1}{4}$ and $\frac{1}{6}$ is A) $\frac{5}{12}$ B) $\frac{1}{5}$ C) $\frac{1}{10}$ D) $\frac{5}{24}$	12. D
13. $\frac{7}{10}$ is *not* equal to A) 70% B) 0.07 C) 0.700 D) $\frac{14}{20}$	13. B
14. Which number is equal to its own reciprocal? A) 0 B) $\frac{1}{2}$ C) $\frac{2}{3}$ D) 1	14. D
15. $3^4 - 2^5 =$ A) 6^2 B) 7^2 C) 7^1 D) 2^5	15. B

Go on to the next page ➠ **7**

16. $\dfrac{5 \times 10 \times 15 \times 20}{5 \times 5 \times 5 \times 5} =$ A) 10 B) 12 C) 24 D) 750	16. C
17. The sum of two whole numbers is 36. Their greatest possible product is A) 35 B) 260 C) 320 D) 324	17. D
18. The product of two whole numbers is 36. Their greatest possible sum is A) 12 B) 13 C) 20 D) 37	18. D
19. $0.5 + \dfrac{5}{100} + \dfrac{1}{4} =$ A) 0.08 B) 8 C) $\dfrac{3}{5}$ D) $\dfrac{4}{5}$	19. D
20. On an \$800 loan (at a 12% annual interest rate), the simple interest for 3 months is A) \$24 B) \$32 C) \$48 D) \$96	20. A
21. Find the area of the figure if all angles are right angles. A) 109 B) 71 C) 99 D) 105	21. D
22. Find the missing number: $(\frac{1}{5})^2 + \frac{4}{5} = (\frac{4}{5})^2 + \underline{\ ?\ }$ A) $\dfrac{4}{25}$ B) $\dfrac{1}{25}$ C) $\dfrac{4}{5}$ D) $\dfrac{1}{5}$	22. D
23. The sum of the digits of a four-digit number can *never* equal A) 1 B) 10 C) 30 D) 40	23. D
24. If 75% of a number is 36, then 150% of the number is A) 18 B) 48 C) 54 D) 72	24. D
25. The perimeter of a rectangle is $\frac{1}{9}$. The sum of the lengths of two adjacent sides is A) $\dfrac{1}{36}$ B) $\dfrac{1}{18}$ C) $\dfrac{2}{3}$ D) $\dfrac{2}{9}$	25. B
26. On segment $\overline{AC}$, $AB = 8$ and $AB:BC = 2:5$. Find AC. A) 20 B) 24 C) 28 D) 40	26. C
27. At 45 km per hour, the time it takes to travel 1 km is A) 180 seconds B) 120 seconds C) 90 seconds D) 80 seconds	27.
28. $1\frac{1}{4}\% =$ A) $\dfrac{5}{4}$ B) $\dfrac{5}{40}$ C) $\dfrac{1}{80}$ D) $\dfrac{4}{500}$	28. A

Go on to the next page ⮕ **7**

| Answers

29. Equilateral triangle *ABC* rests atop square *ACDE*. The measure of angle *BCD* is

A) 30°   B) 60°   C) 90°   D) 150°

29. D

30. One-half of the pupils at Churchill HS walk to school. One-fourth of the remainder go to school by bicycle. What part of the school population travels by neither of these methods?

A) $\frac{1}{8}$ B) $\frac{1}{4}$ C) $\frac{3}{8}$ D) $\frac{5}{8}$

30. C

31. A certain soap is $99\frac{44}{100}\%$ pure. The percent of impurities is

A) $\frac{16}{25}\%$ B) $\frac{33}{50}\%$ C) $\frac{14}{25}\%$ D) $1\frac{44}{100}\%$

31. C

32. The square root of $15 \times 20 \times 12$ is

A) 6   B) 60   C) 80   D) 6000

32. B

33. A sailboat sails 6 km south and then 8 km east. At that moment, how far is the sailboat from its starting point?

A) 10 km   B) 12 km   C) 14 km   D) 48 km

33. A

34. The average of all the whole numbers from 1 to 100 is

A) 49   B) $49\frac{1}{2}$ C) 50   D) $50\frac{1}{2}$

34. D

35. How many squares (each with a perimeter of 12 cm) can be cut from a square whose perimeter is 48 cm?

A) 4   B) 9   C) 12   D) 16

35. D

36. Which choice is the average of the other three choices?

A) 2^5 B) 3^3 C) 5^2 D) $2^2 \times 7$

36. D

37. A whole number is called an *increasing number* if each digit in the number is greater then the digit to its left. For example, 2359 is an increasing number. How many increasing numbers are there between 5000 and 10 000?

A) 3   B) 4   C) 5   D) 6

37. C

38. A circle is inscribed in a square. If the diameter of the circle is 10, what is the area of the square?

A) 40   B) 25   C) 100   D) 400

38. C

39. How many different three-digit numbers can be made using any three of the following five digits: 1, 2, 2, 3, and 3?

A) 12   B) 16   C) 18   D) 20

39. C

40. An ant crawls outside a square of side 1 cm, at all times remaining exactly 1 cm from the boundary of the square. In square cm, the area bounded by one complete circuit of the ant is most nearly equal to

A) 7   B) 8   C) 9   D) 10

40. B

The end of the contest ✍ **7**

1984-85 Annual 7th Grade Contest

Tuesday, February 12, 1985

7

Instructions

- **Time** You will have only *30 minutes* working time for this contest. You might be *unable* to finish all 40 questions in the time allowed.

- **Scores** Remember *this is a contest, not a test*. There is no "passing" or "failing" score. Few students score as high as 30 points (75% correct); students with even half that, 15 points, *deserve commendation!*

- **Format and Point Value** This is a multiple-choice contest. For each question, write the *capital letter* that is *in front of* the answer you choose. For each question, your answer will be one of the *capital letters* A, B, C, or D. Each question you answer correctly is worth 1 point. Unanswered questions receive no credit.

Before Computer

		Answers
1.	Which is an odd whole number? A) 1985×1984 B) 1985×1985 C) 1985×1986 D) $1985\frac{1}{1985}$	1. B
2.	Seventeen hundredths = A) 1700 B) 0.17 C) 0.017 D) 0.0017	2. B
3.	The number of tens in 1000 is A) 3 B) 10 C) 100 D) 1000	3. C
4.	$(17 \times 87) + (17 \times 13) =$ A) 1699 B) 1700 C) 1701 D) 1702	4. B
5.	Which does *not* equal 12 when rounded to the nearest whole number? A) 11.45 B) 11.51 C) 12.18 D) 12.49	5. A
6.	$37.3 - 26.4 =$ A) 11.9 B) 9.9 C) 11.1 D) 10.9	6. D
7.	Mickey Mouse is requested to file 800 cards. If he can file cards at the rate of 80 cards an hour, the number of cards remaining to be filed after 7 hours of work is A) 560 B) 260 C) 240 D) 140	7. C
8.	$\sqrt{1^2 + 2^2 + 2^2} =$ A) 5 B) $\sqrt{5}$ C) 3 D) 9	8. C
9.	In the straight-line diagram, if $m\angle CBD = 36°$, then $m\angle ABD =$ A) 144° B) 324° C) 72° D) 54°	9. A
10.	$\frac{48}{72} =$ A) $\frac{3}{4}$ B) $\frac{5}{8}$ C) 0.65 D) $66\frac{2}{3}\%$	10. D
11.	The number of prime numbers between 35 and 45 is A) 1 B) 2 C) 3 D) 4	11. C
12.	$\frac{3}{2} + \frac{5}{4} + \frac{9}{8} + \frac{18}{16} =$ A) $4\frac{15}{16}$ B) $5\frac{1}{16}$ C) 4 D) 5	12. D
13.	Which of the following is *not* equal to $12\frac{1}{2}\%$? A) 12.5% B) 0.125 C) 12.5 D) $\frac{1}{8}$	13. C
14.	$0.5 \times 0.5 =$ A) $\frac{1}{25}$ B) $\frac{1}{4}$ C) $\frac{1}{5}$ D) $\frac{1}{10}$	14. B
15.	If the circumference of a circle is divided by the length of its diameter, the quotient is A) π B) 2π C) 2 D) 4	15. A

For problem 9 diagram: A   B $\angle 36°$ C, with D above.

16. 400% of 20 equals
A) 20   B) 80   C) 500   D) 8000

16. B

17. How many numbers between 1 and 99 are equal to 4 times an integer?
A) 23   B) 24   C) 25   D) 96

17. B

18. $\frac{0.5}{0.75} =$
A) $\frac{1}{15}$ B) $\frac{3}{15}$ C) $\frac{5}{15}$ D) $\frac{10}{15}$

18. D

19. Of the following numbers, which leaves the largest remainder when divided by 7?
A) 615   B) 305   C) 714   D) 1001

19. A

20. 0.003 =
A) 3%   B) 0.3%   C) 0.03%   D) 0.003%

20. B

21. A rectangle has perimeter 28 cm and area 45 sq. cm. Its dimensions, in centimeters, are
A) 1 and 28   B) 3 and 15   C) 5 and 9   D) 3 and 11

21. C

22. Which is largest?
A) $\frac{5}{8}$ B) $\frac{6}{12}$ C) $\frac{34}{71}$ D) $\frac{4}{9}$

22. A

23. A carton containing one dozen eggs costs 96¢. This is 12¢ less than the cost of twelve individual eggs. One individual egg costs
A) 10¢   B) 9¢   C) 8¢   D) 7¢

23. B

24. $\frac{4\frac{1}{3}}{4} = \frac{?}{12}$
A) 26   B) 13   C) 8   D) 7

24. B

25. If $\frac{3}{4}$ of a number is 24, then $\frac{3}{8}$ of the number is
A) 48   B) 18   C) 12   D) 6

25. C

26. $75\% - 66\frac{2}{3}\% =$
A) $\frac{1}{12}$ B) $\frac{1}{8}$ C) $\frac{1}{6}$ D) $\frac{1}{4}$

26. A

27. Which is greater than $\frac{1}{2}$?
A) 0.49   B) $\frac{5}{0.01}$ C) $3 \times \frac{1}{8}$ D) $\frac{3+6}{18}$

27. B

28. The perimeter of a square and the perimeter of a regular pentagon are equal. If the length of a side of the square is 15 cm, then the length of a side of the pentagon is
A) 3 cm   B) $7\frac{1}{2}$ cm   C) 10 cm   D) 12 cm

28. D

29. $2^4 \times 4^2 =$
A) 6×6 B) 8^6 C) 8^8 D) 4^4

29. D

30. How many whole numbers between 300 and 500 begin and/or end with a 4?

A) 100 B) 110 C) 120 D) 140

30. B

31. The 1985th even positive integer is

A) 1986 B) 3968 C) 3970 D) 3972

31. C

32. If each side of a square is decreased 50%, then the area of the square is decreased

A) 100% B) 75% C) 50% D) 25%

32. B

33. The reciprocal of 1.01 is

A) 0.101 B) 1.01 C) 0.99 D) $\frac{100}{101}$

33. D

34. If 10% of a number is 1 less than 20% of the same number, then 40% of the number equals

A) 4 B) 8 C) 40 D) 80

34. A

35. $\dfrac{\frac{1}{2}+\frac{1}{3}}{1-\frac{1}{2}\times\frac{1}{3}} =$

A) 0 B) 1 C) $\frac{6}{25}$ D) 5

35. B

36. If $\overleftrightarrow{DY}$ bisects right $\angle ABC$, what is the measure of $\angle ABD$?

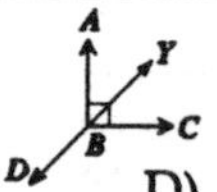

A) 270° B) 45° C) 135° D) 90°

36. C

37. $1985\frac{1}{1985} - 1984\frac{1}{1984}$ most nearly equals

A) 1 B) $\frac{1985}{1984}$ C) $\frac{1984}{1985}$ D) $\frac{1}{1984}$

37. A

38. Five cars (each of the same length) plus eight trucks (each of the same length) take up the same room in a warehouse as 11 trucks. How many cars can fit into a warehouse which can hold 30 trucks?

A) 18 B) 30 C) 50 D) 80

38. C

39. Suppose $a*b = \frac{a+b}{a\times b}$ for any two positive numbers a and b.

Then, $3*4 = \frac{3+4}{3\times 4} = \frac{7}{12}$. What does $(3*4)*5$ equal?

A) $\frac{35}{12}$ B) $\frac{67}{420}$ C) $\frac{1}{35}$ D) $\frac{67}{35}$

39. D

40. Which of the following figures can *not* be folded along the dotted lines to form a cube?

A) 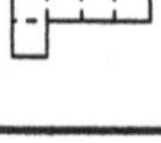 B) 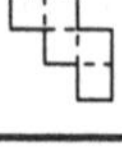 C) 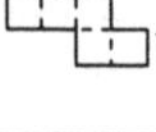 D) 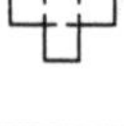

40. D

The end of the contest 7

Perfect

Aug 16/05

Solutions on Page 81 • Answers on Page 148

1985-86 Annual 7th Grade Contest

Tuesday, February 11, 1986

7

Instructions

■ **Time** You will have only *30 minutes* working time for this contest. You might be *unable* to finish all 40 questions in the time allowed.

■ **Scores** Remember *this is a contest, not a test.* There is no "passing" or "failing" score. Few students score as high as 30 points (75% correct); students with even half that, 15 points, *deserve commendation!*

■ **Format and Point Value** This is a multiple-choice contest. For each question, write the *capital letter* that is *in front of* the answer you choose. For each question, your answer will be one of the *capital letters* A, B, C, or D. Each question you answer correctly is worth 1 point. Unanswered questions receive no credit.

Copyright © 1986 by Mathematics Leagues Inc.

13

	Answers
1. Which is equal to 1986? A) $\frac{1986}{1}$ B) $\frac{1986}{1986}$ C) 1987 D) $\frac{1}{1986}$	1.
2. $6666 + 4444 =$ A) 10 000 B) 10 110 C) 11 010 D) 11 110	2.
3. Carol bought 10 pens at 89¢ per pen. She paid for the pens with a \$10 bill. How much change did she receive? A) \$1.10 B) 79¢ C) \$9.11 D) \$2.10	3.
4. $8080 - 7979 =$ A) 111 B) 101 C) 1001 D) 1111	4.
5. Of the following, which is nearest in value to 0.3? A) 50% B) 40% C) 25% D) 20%	5.
6. $4 + 3 \times (8 - 4) =$ A) 52 B) 28 C) 24 D) 16	6.
7. The sum of the measures of any *three* angles of a rectangle is A) 90° B) 180° C) 270° D) 360°	7.
8. $2\frac{2}{3} + \frac{2}{3} =$ A) 2 B) $3\frac{1}{3}$ C) $3\frac{1}{2}$ D) $3\frac{2}{3}$	8.
9. The two prime factors of 511 are 7 and A) 53 B) 63 C) 73 D) 83	9.
10. $0.2 \times 0.2 =$ A) 4 B) $\frac{1}{4}$ C) 0.4 D) 0.04	10.
11. If today is Tuesday, what day will it be 777 days from today? A) Monday B) Tuesday C) Wednesday D) Thursday	11.
12. $\frac{3}{14} \times \frac{7}{15} =$ A) $\frac{2}{5}$ B) $\frac{1}{10}$ C) $\frac{5}{2}$ D) 10	12.
13. Which one of the following *could* be the measure of one of the angles of a right triangle? A) 89° B) 91° C) 93° D) 95°	13.
14. $20 \times 30 \times 40 =$ A) 12×200 B) 24×1000 C) 6×400 D) 40×6000	14.
15. Which is equal to one-tenth of one-tenth? A) $\frac{1}{100}$ B) $\frac{1}{20}$ C) $\frac{1}{5}$ D) 1	15.
16. Which of the following most nearly equals 49.5 divided by 0.5? A) 10 B) 25 C) 50 D) 100	16.

Go on to the next page ⮕ **7**

17. $\frac{99}{999} =$ 17.

   A) $\frac{1}{11}$ B) $\frac{1}{10}$ C) $\frac{1}{9}$ D) $\frac{11}{111}$

18. Find the missing number: $\sqrt{9} \times \sqrt{9} = 9 \times \underline{\ ?\ }$ 18.
   A) 1   B) 3   C) 6   D) 9

19. Which of the following is most nearly equal to 1?   19.
   A) $\frac{99}{100}$ B) $1\frac{1}{99}$ C) 0.9   D) 1.1

20. If a rectangle has an area of 24 m^2 and a perimeter of 20 m, the   20.
   length of one side of the rectangle is
   A) 10 m   B) 8 m   C) 6 m   D) 5 m

21. Region A is $\frac{1}{4}$ of the pie and   21.
   region B is $\frac{1}{3}$ of the pie. What
   part of the pie is region C?

   A) $\frac{1}{2}$ B) $\frac{5}{7}$ C) $\frac{11}{12}$ D) $\frac{5}{12}$

22. $\frac{0.1}{5} =$ 22.

   A) $\frac{1}{50}$ B) $\frac{1}{5}$ C) $\frac{1}{2}$ D) 5

23. Half of the 24 people in a room leave. Then, half of those who   23.
   left return. How many people are now in the room?
   A) 6   B) 12   C) 18   D) 24

24. $5 \times 6 \times 7 \times 8 \times \frac{1}{5} \times \frac{1}{6} \times \frac{1}{7} \times \frac{1}{8} =$ 24.

   A) 0   B) 1   C) 4   D) 8

25. Round 0.999 to the nearest tenth.   25.
   A) 0.1   B) 0.9   C) 0.99   D) 1.0

26. If a tank's gas gauge goes from $\frac{1}{8}$ to $\frac{3}{8}$ when 8 liters are added,   26.
   the capacity of the tank is
   A) 16 liters   B) 24 liters   C) 32 liters   D) 40 liters

27. If 20% of a number is 20, the number itself must be   27.
   A) 4   B) 5   C) 40   D) 100

28. When a pole 30 m tall casts a shadow 15 m long, what would   28.
   be the length of the shadow cast by a 150 m pole?
   A) 3 m   B) 30 m   C) 75 m   D) 135 m

29. $33\frac{1}{3}\%$ of $66\frac{2}{3}\%$ is most nearly equal to   29.

   A) 22%   B) 33%   C) 50%   D) 100%

Go on to the next page ⅢⅢ➡ **7**

30. There are 15 boys and 21 girls in a classroom. How many girls must leave the room so there will then be 3 times as many boys in the room as girls in the room?

    A) 5   B) 6   C) 16   D) 18

    30.

31. If the area of rectangle *ABCD* is 24, then the area of triangle *AED* is

    A) 16   B) 15   C) 12   D) 6

    31.

32. The greatest possible number of Mondays that can occur during a period of 45 consecutive days is

    A) 5   B) 6   C) 7   D) 9

    32.

33. If ■ × ■ + ▼ = ▼, then ■ =

    A) -1   B) 0   C) $\frac{1}{2}$ D) 1

    33.

34. The average of three numbers is 67. If two of the numbers are 56 and 91, the third number is

    A) 34   B) 44   C) 52   D) 54

    34.

35. The difference between two prime numbers is 1985. The larger of these two prime numbers is

    A) 2431   B) 2002   C) 1987   D) 1986

    35.

36. When a number is added to one-third of itself, the result is 60. The number is

    A) 40   B) 45   C) 80   D) 180

    36.

37. A circular pizza of radius 8 is cut into 8 equal slices. The perimeter of one slice is

    A) $16 + 2\pi$ B) 2π C) 8π D) $8 + 4\pi$

    37.

38. If each side of a square is increased by 50%, the area of the square is increased by

    A) 50%   B) 100%   C) 125%   D) 225%

    38.

39. $2^7 \times 5^6 =$

    A) 2 000 000   B) 1 280 000   C) 2 555 555   D) 5 200 200

    39.

40. The symbol $n!$ means the product of all the natural numbers from 1 through n. For example, $4! = 4\times3\times2\times1 = 24$. The units' digit of $11! + 10! + 9! + 8! + 7! + 6! + 5! + 4! + 3! + 2!$ is

    A) 0   B) 1   C) 2   D) 3

    40.

The end of the contest 🖐 **7**

Solutions on Page 85 • Answers on Page 149

1986-87 Annual 7th Grade Contest

Tuesday, February 10, 1987

7

Instructions

- **Time** You will have only *30 minutes* working time for this contest. You might be *unable* to finish all 40 questions in the time allowed.

- **Scores** Remember *this is a contest, not a test.* There is no "passing" or "failing" score. Few students score as high as 30 points (75% correct); students with even half that, 15 points, *deserve commendation!*

- **Format and Point Value** This is a multiple-choice contest. For each question, write the *capital letter* that is *in front of* the answer you choose. For each question, your answer will be one of the *capital letters* A, B, C, or D. Each question you answer correctly is worth 1 point. Unanswered questions receive no credit.

	Answers
1. Which one of the following is an *odd* number? A) 1+9+87 B) 1×98×7 C) 198^7 D) 19+87	1.
2. $3^2 + 4^2 - 5^2 =$ A) 0 B) 2 C) 4 D) 8	2.
3. The product of 3, 4, and 5 equals the sum of 4 × 5 and A) 3 B) 3 × 5 C) 8 D) 8 × 5	3.
4. $\frac{6}{7} \times \frac{7}{8} \times \frac{8}{9} =$ A) $\frac{1}{3}$ B) $\frac{2}{3}$ C) $\frac{6}{504}$ D) 1	4.
5. The sum of two numbers is 100. One of the numbers is 2 more than the other. The larger number is A) 50 B) 51 C) 52 D) 53	5.
6. Each of the following is equal to $\frac{3}{5}$ *except* A) $\frac{6}{10}$ B) $\frac{33}{55}$ C) 60% D) 0.06	6.
7. In an isosceles triangle, the largest angle is a 100° angle. The number of degrees in each of the other angles is A) 40° B) 50° C) 80° D) 180°	7.
8. 225% = A) $\frac{225}{1000}$ B) $\frac{1}{4}$ C) 22.5 D) $2\frac{1}{4}$	8.
9. A bell rings every 2 seconds and a bird chirps every 3 seconds. If the ring and the chirp occur together right now, they will also occur together in A) 40 seconds B) 41 seconds C) 42 seconds D) 43 seconds	9.
10. Find the missing number: $\frac{1}{4} + \frac{3}{4} = \frac{1}{2} + \frac{?}{2}$. A) 1 B) 2 C) 3 D) 4	10.
11. $\frac{0.55}{2} =$ A) 1.10 B) 27.5 C) 2.75 D) 0.275	11.
12. Which of the following is a prime number? A) 1985 B) 1986 C) 1987 D) 1988	12.
13. $(5 \times \frac{1}{1000}) + (4 \times \frac{1}{100}) + (3 \times \frac{1}{10}) =$ A) 0.345 B) 0.435 C) 0.534 D) 0.543	13.
14. A rectangle with dimensions 4 by 9 has the same area as a square. The perimeter of the square is A) 6 B) 24 C) 26 D) 36	14.
15. If 10 zigs = 6 zags, then 1 zig = A) $\frac{3}{5}$ zags B) $\frac{2}{3}$ zags C) $1\frac{3}{5}$ zags D) $1\frac{2}{3}$ zags	15.

16.	1 second is what fractional part of 1 hour? A) $\frac{1}{7200}$ B) $\frac{1}{3600}$ C) $\frac{1}{1440}$ D) $\frac{1}{60}$	16.
17.	When 0.48 is divided by 0.016, the quotient is A) 0.3 B) 3 C) 30 D) 300	17.
18.	The average of 3 numbers is between 7 and 10. The sum of the numbers could be any of the following *except* A) 20 B) 22 C) 26 D) 28	18.
19.	Which of the following is the smallest number? A) $\frac{99}{197}$ B) $\frac{1}{2}$ C) $\frac{49}{99}$ D) $\frac{100}{199}$	19.
20.	On a scale drawing, 2 centimeters represent 50 meters. How many centimeters represent 5 meters? A) 10 B) 0.02 C) 0.2 D) $\frac{1}{10}$	20.
21.	The measures of the angles of a triangle are consecutive integers. The measure of the *smallest* angle is A) 1° B) 59° C) 60° D) 180°	21.
22.	$\frac{1}{3}$ equals the product of $\frac{3}{4}$ and A) $\frac{1}{4}$ B) $\frac{9}{4}$ C) $\frac{5}{12}$ D) $\frac{4}{9}$	22.
23.	Which of the following has the *largest* value? A) $2 \times [9 - (6 - 3)]$ B) $2 \times [(9 - 6) - 3]$ C) $[2 \times (9 - 6)] - 3$ D) $(2 \times 9) - (6 - 3)$	23.
24.	When 18 is divided by $4\frac{1}{2}$, the quotient is A) $\frac{1}{81}$ B) $\frac{1}{4}$ C) 4 D) 81	24.
25.	An isosceles triangle has two sides whose lengths are 2 and 8. The perimeter of this triangle is A) 10 B) 12 C) 18 D) 22	25.
26.	How many eighths are there in $5\frac{3}{4}$? A) 46 B) 43 C) 40 D) 6	26.
27.	How many more cartons are needed to hold 1500 books in cartons of 10 than in cartons of 15? A) 5 B) 50 C) 100 D) 500	27.
28.	If $a \blacktriangle b = a + a + b + b$, then $2 \blacktriangle 3 =$ A) 6 B) 10 C) 12 D) 13	28.
29.	$\left(\left(\left(\frac{1}{2} \div \frac{1}{3}\right) \div \frac{1}{4}\right) \div \frac{1}{4}\right) =$ A) $\frac{1}{48}$ B) 24 C) 48 D) 96	29.

30. In which of the following number pairs is the second number greater than the square of the first? A) 0, 0 B) $\frac{1}{3}, \frac{1}{3}$ C) $\frac{1}{2}, \frac{1}{4}$ D) $\frac{1}{2}, 0$	30.
31. Find the missing number: $\frac{10}{14} = \sqrt{\frac{25}{?}}$. A) 7 B) 35 C) 49 D) 196	31.
32. In a club of 24 members, every person serves on four 3-person committees. How many committees are there? A) 32 B) 24 C) 18 D) 12	32.
33. If B is the midpoint of $\overline{AC}$, and if C is the midpoint of $\overline{BD}$, then what percent of CD is AC? A) 25% B) 50% C) 100% D) 200%	33.
34. In a class of students, the ratio of those under 12 years old to those 12 or over is 2 to 3. In this class, the percent of students 12 or over is A) $33\frac{1}{3}\%$ B) 40% C) 60% D) $66\frac{2}{3}\%$	34.
35. The product of a certain integer and 12 is the *square* of an integer. Which is always a factor of the original integer? A) 2 B) 3 C) 4 D) 12	35.
36. The volume of cube I is 331 m^3 less than the volume if cube II. If an edge of cube I is 10 meters, an edge of cube II is A) 14 meters B) 13 meters C) 12 meters D) 11 meters	36.
37. Which of the following has the largest reciprocal? A) $\sqrt{64}$ B) 64 C) 64^2 D) 64^3	37.
38. A wheel with a diameter of 2 meters rolls on the street for 100 meters. Most nearly, the wheel made _?_ complete revolutions. A) 64 B) 32 C) 16 D) 8	38.
39. I worked twice as long as Ron and 3 times as long as Mary. We all earned the same hourly wage. Together, we earned less than $125. Of the following, the most I could have earned was A) $54 B) $60 C) $66 D) $72	39.
40. Action Comic #1, which originally sold for 10¢, now sells for $18 500. This comic has increased in value A) 18 500 000% B) 185 000% C) 1 849 990% D) 18 499 900%	40.

The end of the contest 🖎 **7**

Solutions on Page 89 • Answers on Page 150

1987-88 Annual 7th Grade Contest

Tuesday, February 2, 1988

Instructions

- **Time** You will have only *30 minutes* working time for this contest. You might be *unable* to finish all 40 questions in the time allowed.

- **Scores** Remember *this is a contest, not a test.* There is no "passing" or "failing" score. Few students score as high as 30 points (75% correct); students with even half that, 15 points, *deserve commendation!*

- **Format and Point Value** This is a multiple-choice contest. For each question, write the *capital letter* that is *in front of* the answer you choose. For each question, your answer will be one of the *capital letters* A, B, C, or D. Each question you answer correctly is worth 1 point. Unanswered questions receive no credit.

21

| 1. | 100 quarters = _?_ dollars | | | | 1. |
| | A) 4 | B) 25 | C) 40 | D) 2500 | |

2. $1988 - \frac{1987}{1988} =$ **2.**
A) $1988\frac{1}{1988}$ B) $1988\frac{1987}{1988}$ C) $1987\frac{1}{1988}$ D) $1987\frac{1987}{1988}$

3. 0% of $\frac{44}{7}$ is **3.**
A) $\frac{44}{7}$ B) $\frac{22}{7}$ C) $\frac{11}{7}$ D) $\frac{0}{7}$

4. Doing homework, Pat spent 20 minutes on English, 25 minutes on math, 20 minutes on science, and 15 minutes on social studies. The total time Pat spent doing homework was **4.**
A) $1\frac{1}{5}$ hours   B) $1\frac{1}{4}$ hours   C) $1\frac{1}{3}$ hours   D) $1\frac{1}{2}$ hours

5. When $\frac{1}{4}$ is divided by $\frac{1}{8}$, the quotient is **5.**
A) 32   B) 2   C) $\frac{1}{2}$ D) $\frac{1}{32}$

6. $\sqrt{25 \times 25} =$ **6.**
A) 625   B) 25   C) 10   D) 5

7. In triangle ABC, angle C is a 60° angle. If $AC = BC = 5$, then the measure of angle B is **7.** 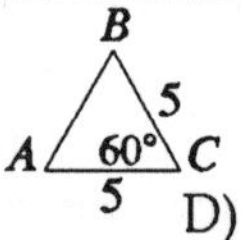
A) 60°   B) 45°   C) 30°   D) 12°

8. 50% of $\frac{1}{6}$ is **8.**
A) $\frac{1}{2}$ B) $\frac{1}{3}$ C) $\frac{1}{9}$ D) $\frac{1}{12}$

9. A rectangular lot measures 42 m by 26 m. If I walk around the boundary of this lot once, I'll have walked a total distance of **9.**
A) 68 m   B) 104 m   C) 136 m   D) 272 m

10. 22% of 99 = 99% of **10.**
A) 0.22   B) 2.2   C) 22   D) 220

11. 50.050 − 0.005 = **11.**
A) 50.045   B) 50.055   C) 49.945   D) 49.045

12. $\frac{88}{88} - \frac{19}{19} =$ **12.**
A) 0   B) 1   C) $\frac{69}{88}$ D) $\frac{69}{19}$

13. In the diagram, the perimeter of the larger square is 20 and the perimeter of the smaller square is 16. The area of the region between the two squares is **13.** 
A) 1   B) 2   C) 4   D) 9

14. $\frac{1}{6} + \underline{\ ?\ } = \frac{1}{2}$ **14.**
A) $\frac{1}{4}$ B) $\frac{1}{3}$ C) $\frac{1}{2}$ D) $\frac{1}{6}$

15. If the sum of 8.34 and 7.13 is rounded to the nearest tenth, the result is A) 15.47 B) 15.4 C) 15.5 D) 20	15.
16. When 10% is divided by 100, the quotient is A) $\frac{1}{1000}$ B) $\frac{1}{100}$ C) $\frac{1}{10}$ D) 10	16.
17. If a fortnight is two weeks, then 44 fortnights is A) 88 days B) 154 days C) 308 days D) 616 days	17.
18. $3 \times (\frac{5}{3} + \frac{7}{3} + \frac{9}{3}) =$ A) 7 B) 21 C) 63 D) $\frac{7}{3}$	18.
19. On a map, 2 cm represents 50 km. The distance between two towns on this map is 7.5 cm. Their actual distance apart is A) 375 km B) 275 km C) 187.5 km D) 75 km	19.
20. $\frac{1}{2} \times \frac{1}{4} \times 9876 = \frac{1}{8} \times \underline{\ ?\ }$ A) 9876 B) 4938 C) 2469 D) 1234	20.
21. In the diagram, triangle *ABC* is an equilateral triangle. The sum of the measures of the angles marked 1 and 2 is A) 60° B) 90° C) 120° D) 180°	21.
22. The sum of a positive number and its reciprocal is *always* A) 0 B) 1 C) 2 D) more than 1.9	22.
23. When Jan bought a TV, the ticket price was 10% below the $180 list price. Because of a holiday sale, the cashier reduced the ticket price by 20%. Jan's cost for the TV was A) $162 B) $129.60 C) $126 D) $120	23.
24. The number of eighths in 7.75 is A) 10 B) 31 C) 59 D) 62	24.
25. A number is multiplied by 5, then divided by 6. The result is $\frac{3}{8}$. The original number was A) $\frac{5}{16}$ B) $\frac{5}{6}$ C) $\frac{6}{5}$ D) $\frac{9}{20}$	25.
26. If Pat has $2.48, then Pat has at most _?_ nickels. A) 9 B) 49 C) 50 D) 245	26.
27. The ratio of $\frac{1}{2}$ to 8 is equivalent to A) 1:16 B) 1:6 C) 2:$\frac{1}{8}$ D) $\frac{1}{2}$:4	27.
28. The area of the shaded region of the rectangle is A) 6 B) 12 C) 28 D) 34	28.

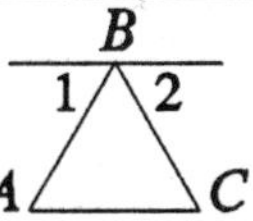

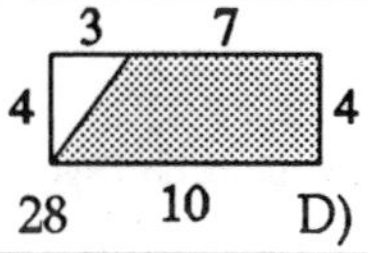

23   *Go on to the next page* ⫸   **7**

29. Which of the following is the largest? A) $(0.3)^2$ B) $\sqrt{0.09}$ C) 0.5×0.5 D) .09	29.
30. The area of a rectangle with dimensions of 30 cm and 20 cm is A) 0.06 m^2 B) 0.6 m^2 C) 6 m^2 D) 600 m^2	30.
31. What number must be added to both the numerator and the denominator of $\frac{1}{3}$ to make the value of the resulting fraction $\frac{2}{3}$? A) 1 B) 2 C) 3 D) 4	31.
32. If the average of 3 numbers is between 5 and 8, then their sum *cannot* be A) $15\frac{1}{3}$ B) 16 C) $20\frac{3}{4}$ D) 25	32.
33. $[(0.3)^2 + (0.4)^2]^2 =$ A) 25 B) 6.25 C) 0.625 D) 0.0625	33.
34. $\sqrt{\sqrt{16}} =$ A) 1 B) 2 C) 4 D) 8	34.
35. $28 \times 5\frac{1}{2} =$ A) $(28 \times 50) + (28 \times \frac{1}{2})$ B) $(20 \times 5) + (8 \times 5) + (28 \times \frac{1}{2})$ C) $(20 \times 50) + (8 \times 5\frac{1}{2})$ D) $(28 \times \frac{1}{2}) + (8 \times 5\frac{1}{2}) + (20 \times 5)$	35.
36. If neither triangle T nor parallelogram P has any vertex on a side of the other figure, then T and P can intersect in at most A) 3 points B) 4 points C) 5 points D) 6 points	36.
37. 999^2 is between A) 10^3 and 10^4 B) 10^4 and 10^5 C) 10^5 and 10^6 D) 10^6 and 10^7	37.
38. The sum of the first 1 million primes is N. Without knowing N's value, one can determine that the ones' digit of N cannot be A) 1 B) 2 C) 3 D) 9	38.
39. The tens' digit of $65 \times 76 \times 87 \times 98 \times 109 \times 120 \times 131 \times 142$ is A) 0 B) 5 C) 7 D) 9	39.
40. The nth triangular number is defined to be the sum of the first n positive whole numbers. For example, since $1 + 2 + 3 = 6$, the 3rd triangular number is 6. If the 100th triangular number is 5050, then the 101st triangular number is A) 5051 B) 5150 C) 5151 D) 5250	40.

The end of the contest ✍️ **7**

Solutions on Page 93 • Answers on Page 151

1988-89 Annual 7th Grade Contest

Tuesday, February 7, 1989

7

Instructions

■ **Time** You will have only *30 minutes* working time for this contest. You might be *unable* to finish all 40 questions in the time allowed.

■ **Scores** Remember *this is a contest, not a test.* There is no "passing" or "failing" score. Few students score as high as 30 points (75% correct); students with even half that, 15 points, *deserve commendation!*

■ **Format and Point Value** This is a multiple-choice contest. For each question, write the *capital letter* that is *in front of* the answer you choose. For each question, your answer will be one of the *capital letters* A, B, C, or D. Each question you answer correctly is worth 1 point. Unanswered questions receive no credit.

1988-89 7TH GRADE CONTEST

	Answers
1. 9876 + 543 + 21 = A) 10100 B) 12340 C) 10340 D) 10440	1.
2. Of the following, which is largest? A) $\frac{1989}{1987}$ B) $\frac{1989}{1988}$ C) $\frac{1989}{1989}$ D) $\frac{1989}{1990}$	2.
3. What is the quotient when 20 is divided by 0.2? A) 0.1 B) 1 C) 10 D) 100	3.
4. The average number of degrees in an angle in a triangle is A) 45° B) 60° C) 90° D) 180°	4.
5. $1 - 0.1 - 0.01 =$ A) 0.98 B) 0.91 C) 0.89 D) 0.8	5.
6. To the nearest 1%, what percent of the letters in the word "facetious" are vowels? A) 50% B) 56% C) 63% D) 67%	6.
7. $\sqrt{(1\times9) + (8\times9)} =$ A) 3 B) 9 C) 40.5 D) 81	7.
8. $3\frac{5}{8} =$ A) $\frac{29}{16}$ B) $\frac{34}{16}$ C) $\frac{58}{16}$ D) $\frac{53}{16}$	8.
9. Which product represents the greatest number? A) $2\times22\times22$ B) $22\times22\times22$ C) 22×222 D) 2×2222	9.
10. Which is equal to 0.11? A) $\frac{1}{9}$ B) $\frac{10}{11}$ C) $\frac{11}{100}$ D) $\frac{1}{11}$	10.
11. $5 \div (5 \div 5) =$ A) 0.2 B) 1 C) 5 D) 25	11.
12. The sum of _?_ and its reciprocal equals 2. A) 2.5 B) 2 C) 1 D) 0.5	12.
13. $\frac{3}{2}\times\frac{4}{3}\times\frac{5}{4}\times\frac{6}{5}\times\frac{7}{6}\times\frac{8}{7} =$ A) 4 B) 6 C) 7 D) 8	13.
14. $2^3 + 2^3 =$ A) 64 B) 16 C) 12 D) 8	14.
15. Round 996.47 to the nearest whole number. A) 996 B) 997 C) 996.4 D) 996.5	15.
16. $0.758 - \frac{3}{4} =$ A) 0.008 B) 0.683 C) 0.75 D) 0.8	16.

Go on to the next page ➡ **7**

17. In the proportion 10 : 100 = 1000 : _?_, the missing number is | 17.
    A) 10   B) 100   C) 1000   D) 10000

18. Of the following number pairs, the fewest primes lie between | 18.
    A) 0 and 10   B) 10 and 20   C) 20 and 30   D) 40 and 50

19. $(\frac{2}{5} \times \frac{1}{7}) + (\frac{1}{5} \times \frac{2}{7}) =$ | 19.
    A) $\frac{1}{5} \times \frac{1}{7}$ B) $\frac{2}{5} \times \frac{2}{7}$ C) $\frac{3}{5} \times \frac{3}{7}$ D) $\frac{2}{25} \times \frac{2}{49}$

20. The length of the line segment joining the centers of two congruent circles is 12. What is the length of a diameter of one of these circles? | 20.

    A) 6   B) 12   C) 24   D) 36

21. $2 \times 3 \times (\frac{1}{2} + \frac{1}{3}) =$ | 21.
    A) 1   B) 2   C) 5   D) 6

22. Of the following, which has a value that most nearly equals 10? | 22.
    A) $\frac{66.7}{6.7}$ B) $\frac{66.7}{67}$ C) $\frac{667}{0.67}$ D) $\frac{667}{6.7}$

23. My average on 5 tests is 80. If my lowest grade is dropped, my average on the 4 remaining tests is 86. My lowest grade was | 23.
    A) 56   B) 62   C) 66   D) 74

24. 1 m + 1 cm = | 24.
    A) 1.01 m   B) 1.1 m   C) 1.11 m   D) 101 m

25. Each of the following can be expressed as the sum of two *consecutive* whole numbers *except* | 25.
    A) 2   B) 3   C) 5   D) 1989

26. The number 1 is what percent of the number 2.5? | 26.
    A) 20%   B) $\frac{2}{5}$%   C) $\frac{5}{2}$%   D) 40%

27. The average area of the three triangles drawn inside the 4 by 9 rectangle at the right is | 27.

    A) 6   B) 8   C) 12   D) 18

28. A repeating decimal can be written in another way, by using a bar over the digits that repeat. Thus, $0.\overline{123}$ means 0.123123 .... The sum of the repeating decimals $0.\overline{123}$, $0.\overline{231}$, and $0.\overline{312}$ is | 28.
    A) 0.66   B) $\frac{6}{10}$ C) $\frac{2}{3}$ D) 0.6666666

29. A rectangle is formed from a string 28 cm long. The largest possible area that this rectangle could have is | 29.
    A) 24 cm^2 B) 48 cm^2 C) 49 cm^2 D) 56 cm^2

30. If an ant can carry 5 times its weight, then how many ants, each weighing 0.001 kg would be needed to together carry a weight equal to the weight of a 2000 kg car?
    A) 10   B) 400 000   C) 4 million   D) 10 million
    30.

31. I'm thinking of a prime number greater than 5. When I add 2 to this number, I get another prime. When I add 2 to the second prime, I'll always get a number that
    A) is even   B) is prime   C) ends in 5   D) is odd
    31.

32. Of the following, which has the smallest value?
    A) $\frac{\pi}{2}\times\frac{\pi}{3}$ B) $\frac{\pi}{2}\times\frac{\pi}{3}\times\frac{\pi}{4}$ C) $\frac{\pi}{3}\times\frac{\pi}{4}\times\frac{\pi}{5}$ D) $\frac{\pi}{4}\times\frac{\pi}{5}$
    32.

33. When I divide two numbers by 7, the respective remainders are 2 and 4. The product of the two numbers could be
    A) 148   B) 147   C) 146   D) 145
    33.

34. I set my watch correctly at 9 A.M., but it ran 9 minutes fast every real hour. When 9 real hours had passed, my watch read
    A) 9:21 P.M.   B) 7:21 P.M.   C) 6:09 P.M.   D) 4:39 P.M.
    34.

35. If low-fat yogurt has 25% fewer calories than regular yogurt, and if a container of low-fat yogurt has 180 calories, then the same-sized container of regular yogurt contains _?_ calories.
    A) 135   B) 205   C) 225   D) 240
    35.

36. I can purchase 3 cassettes for the price of 2 CD's. If I buy 3 CD's and 6 cassettes for $84, then the price of one CD is
    A) $10   B) $11   C) $12   D) $13
    36.

37. A number which is divisible by *only* 3 of the 4 numbers listed in the choices given for this problem will *not* be divisible by
    A) 6   B) 10   C) 14   D) 15
    37.

38. At 3:30, the hands of an accurate school clock make an angle of
    A) 90°   B) 75°   C) 65°   D) 60°
    38.

39. In a group of 31 people, how many different handshakes will occur if each person shakes hands just once with everyone else?
    A) 15×31   B) 30×30   C) 30×31   D) 31×31
    39.

40. For what value of x will the sum of the numbers in each row, each column, and both major diagonals be equal in the "magic square" shown at the right?

13		4	
8	10	17	
		5	6	12
		x		9

    A) 14   B) 15   C) 16   D) 18
    40.

The end of the contest ✍️ **7**

Solutions on Page 97 • Answers on Page 152

28

1989-90 Annual 7th Grade Contest

Tuesday, February 6, 1990

7

Instructions

- **Time** You will have only *30 minutes* working time for this contest. You might be *unable* to finish all 40 questions in the time allowed.

- **Scores** Remember *this is a contest, not a test*. There is no "passing" or "failing" score. Few students score as high as 30 points (75% correct); students with even half that, 15 points, *deserve commendation!*

- **Format and Point Value** This is a multiple-choice contest. For each question, write the *capital letter* that is *in front of* the answer you choose. For each question, your answer will be one of the *capital letters* A, B, C, or D. Each question you answer correctly is worth 1 point. Unanswered questions receive no credit.

Copyright © 1990 by Mathematics Leagues Inc.

1. The total value of five pennies, five nickels, and five dimes is
   A) 15¢   B) 60¢   C) 70¢   D) 80¢

   1.

2. Find the missing number: 1990 = 199 × ?
   A) 0   B) 10   C) 100   D) 1000

   2.

3. Today, Uncle Joe is 68 years old. What is the difference between his age today and his age 50 years ago?
   A) 18 years   B) 40 years   C) 50 years   D) 68 years

   3.

4. $\frac{1}{5} + \frac{2}{10} + \frac{3}{15} + \frac{4}{20} =$
   A) $\frac{4}{5}$ B) 1   C) $1\frac{1}{5}$ D) $1\frac{2}{5}$

   4.

5. Of the following numbers, which is the largest?
   A) 0.0099   B) 0.02   C) 0.0111   D) 0.1

   5.

6. Find the missing number:
   10 + 10 + 10 + 10 + 10 + 10 + 10 + 10 + 10 = 10×10 − ?
   A) 0   B) 1   C) 9   D) 10

   6.

7. How many positive prime numbers are divisible by 3?
   A) 0   B) 1   C) 3   D) 9

   7.

8. 1.11 − 0.999 =
   A) 0.111   B) 0.888   C) 1.111   D) 2.109

   8.

9. Boatman can travel in his Boatmobile at 80 km/hr. At that rate of speed, how long would it take Boatman to travel 40 km?
   A) $\frac{1}{2}$ minute   B) 30 minutes   C) 40 minutes   D) 2 hours

   9.

10. Find the missing number: 4×6×8×10 = 2×3×4×5× ?
    A) 2   B) 6   C) 8   D) 16

    10.

11. Parallelogram *ABCD* will be a rhombus whenever

    A) *AB = CD*   B) *AB = BA*   C) *AB = AD*   D) *BC = AD*

    11.

12. Find the missing number: $\frac{2}{3} = \underline{\ ?\ } \times \frac{4}{3}$
    A) $\frac{1}{2}$ B) $\frac{2}{3}$ C) $\frac{4}{3}$ D) 2

    12.

13. Which of the following is equal to 12?
    A) 3+2×3+3   B) 2+3×2+2   C) 1+3×1+2   D) 1+3×3×1

    13.

14. When 4 is divided by $\frac{1}{4}$, the quotient equals
    A) $\frac{1}{16}$ B) 1   C) $\frac{17}{4}$ D) 16

    14.

15. If a three-digit number is 50 more than some two-digit number, what is the largest possible value of this three-digit number?
    A) 149   B) 150   C) 151   D) 999

    15.

Go on to the next page ⮕ **7**

16. $0.02 \times 0.05 =$ A) 0.1 B) 0.01 C) 0.001 D) 0.0001	16.
17. The sum of the two acute angles in a right triangle is A) 60° B) 90° C) 120° D) 180°	17.
18. Round 0.0049 to the nearest hundredth. A) 0.00 B) 0.004 C) 0.005 D) 0.01	18.
19. If $1234 - (1 + 10 + 100 + 1000) = 1234 - \underline{?}$, then $\underline{?} =$ A) 111 B) 123 C) 234 D) 1111	19.
20. What is 50% of $\frac{1}{50}$? A) 0.01 B) 1 C) 0.25 D) 0.04	20.
21. $(0.1 \times 0.2 \times 0.3) - (\frac{1}{10} \times \frac{2}{10} \times \frac{3}{10}) =$ A) 0 B) 1 C) 0.246 D) 0.594	21.
22. If twice the length of a diameter of a circle is 24, what is the length of a radius of this circle? A) 12 B) 6 C) 3 D) 1	22.
23. $\frac{1}{10} + \frac{1}{5} + \frac{1}{10} + \frac{1}{5} + \frac{1}{10} + \frac{1}{5} + \frac{1}{10} + \frac{1}{5} =$ A) $\frac{7}{10}$ B) $\frac{4}{5}$ C) 1 D) $\frac{6}{5}$	23.
24. What is the average of the two primes nearest in value to 38? A) 37 B) 38 C) 39 D) 40	24.
25. $22:44 =$ A) 44:22 B) 33:55 C) 11:33 D) 44:88	25.
26. Two congruent equilateral triangles form quadrilateral *ABCD* as shown. The perimeter of each triangle is 24. What is the perimeter of quadrilateral *ABCD*? A) 24 B) 32 C) 40 D) 48	26.
27. Find the missing number: $\sqrt{1} + \sqrt{4} + \sqrt{9} + \sqrt{16} = \sqrt{?}$. A) 10 B) 25 C) 30 D) 100	27.
28. What is the correct time 59 minutes before 10:56 A.M.? A) 11:57 A.M. B) 9:59 A.M. C) 9:57 A.M. D) 10:01 A.M.	28.
29. $10^2 - 1 =$ A) 9×9 B) 9×10 C) 9×11 D) 19	29.
30. 1 km = A) 10^6 cm B) 10^5 cm C) 10^4 cm D) 10^3 cm	30.

Go on to the next page **7**

31

	Answers
31. The sun is about 140 million km away. If I drove my car as fast as possible, I'd go about 700 thousand km per year. If it were possible to drive directly to the sun, and I drove as fast as I could, how long would it take me to reach the sun? A) 2 years B) 20 years C) 200 years D) 2000 years	31.
32. $3^2 + 4^2 + 3^2 + 4^2 + 3^2 + 4^2 + 3^2 + 4^2 =$ A) 10^2 B) 14^2 C) 20^2 D) 28^2	32.
33. In a special election the winner must receive at least $\frac{2}{3}$ of the total votes cast. If 1001 people voted, what's the least number of votes that a candidate would need to win this election? A) 601 B) 666 C) 667 D) 668	33.
34. The sum of seven consecutive whole numbers is 77. The largest of these whole numbers is A) 7 B) 11 C) 14 D) 17	34.
35. In a right triangle, the *square* of the length of one leg is 16 and the *square* of the length of the hypotenuse is 20. What is the *length* of the other leg? A) 2 B) 4 C) 6 D) 36	35.
36. A truck uses 3.5 tanks of gas to drive 560 km. How many tanks of gas would this truck use to drive 640 km? A) 4 B) 4.5 C) 6 D) 11.5	36.
37. Let $\S(d)\S = \frac{d}{d+1}$. What is the value of $\S(\S(1)\S)\S$? A) $\frac{1}{2}$ B) $\frac{1}{3}$ C) $\frac{1}{4}$ D) $\frac{2}{3}$	37.
38. John's age is $\frac{2}{5}$ of Pat's age, but $\frac{3}{4}$ of Mary's age. The ratio of Pat's age to Mary's age is A) 3:15 B) 8:15 C) 15:8 D) 10:3	38.
39. Any 50-digit whole number which ends in . . . 360 must always be divisible by A) 9 B) 8 C) 6 D) 3	39.
40. When the product of the first 1001 positive primes is divided by the product of the first 1000 positive primes, the quotient must be A) 1000 B) 1001 C) prime D) even	40.

The end of the contest ✍️ **7**

Solutions on Page 101 • Answers on Page 153

1990-91 Annual 7th Grade Contest

Tuesday, February 5, 1991

7

Instructions

- **Time** You will have only *30 minutes* working time for this contest. You might be *unable* to finish all 40 questions in the time allowed.

- **Scores** Remember *this is a contest, not a test.* There is no "passing" or "failing" score. Few students score as high as 30 points (75% correct); students with even half that, 15 points, *deserve commendation!*

- **Format and Point Value** This is a multiple-choice contest. For each question, write the *capital letter* that is *in front of* the answer you choose. For each question, your answer will be one of the *capital letters* A, B, C, or D. Each question you answer correctly is worth 1 point. Unanswered questions receive no credit.

Answers

1. Find the missing number: $19 \times 91 = 91 \times \underline{\ ?\ }$ A) 9 B) 19 C) 91 D) 1991	1.
2. 1 fortnight = 2 weeks = $\underline{\ ?\ }$ days A) 4 B) 7 C) 8 D) 14	2.
3. $\frac{1}{1} + \frac{22}{22} + \frac{333}{333} =$ A) 1 B) 3 C) 6 D) 356	3.
4. Ice cream pops cost 75¢ each and ice cream cones cost 95¢ each. What is the cost of 4 pops and 2 cones? A) $1.20 B) $3.00 C) $4.90 D) $6.00	4.
5. Of the following numbers, which is closest to 99.4? A) 99 B) 100 C) 101 D) 102	5.
6. $\sqrt{1 \times 9 \times 9 \times 1} =$ A) 3 B) 9 C) 81 D) 1991	6.
7. How many degrees does the minute hand of a circular clock move in 1 hour? A) 1° B) 60° C) 120° D) 360°	7.
8. $1^1 \times 1^2 \times 1^3 \times \ldots \times 1^{100} =$ A) 0 B) 1 C) 10 D) 100	8.
9. The perimeter of an equilateral triangle is 36. What is the length of a side of this triangle? A) 6 B) 12 C) 18 D) 36	9.
10. $3.141 \div 0.9 =$ A) $\pi \div 0.9$ B) 3.39 C) 3.49 D) 3.59	10.
11. The sum of the six whole number factors of 32 is A) 30 B) 31 C) 32 D) 63	11.
12. $1000 \times 0.0001 =$ A) 1 B) 0.1 C) 0.01 D) 0.001	12.
13. $\frac{5 \times 4 \times 3 \times 2 \times 1}{1 \times 2 \times 3 \times 4 \times 5} =$ A) 1 B) 5 C) 24 D) 120	13.
14. $0.1 + 0.2 + 0.3 + 0.4 =$ A) 1% B) 10% C) 100% D) 1000%	14.
15. 1 centimeter = A) 100 m B) 10 m C) 0.1 m D) 0.01 m	15.

Go on to the next page ➡ **7**

Answers

16. $\frac{46 \times 4}{23 \times 2} =$

A) 2   B) 4   C) 23   D) 46

16.

17. If $1 Canadian = 80¢ U.S., then $1 U.S. = _?_ Canadian.

A) $1.25   B) $1.20   C) 80¢   D) 75¢

17.

18. Which of the following inequalities is *false*?

A) $\frac{10}{11} < \frac{29}{33}$ B) $\frac{4}{5} < \frac{25}{30}$ C) $\frac{3}{7} < \frac{16}{35}$ D) $\frac{7}{13} < \frac{22}{39}$

18.

19. The average of the first ten positive whole numbers is

A) 5   B) 5.5   C) 6   D) 10

19.

20. $\frac{3}{4}\% =$

A) 0.75   B) 0.075   C) 0.0075   D) 0.00075

20.

21. $10 \times 10 \times 10 \times 0.1 \times 0.1 \times 0.1 =$

A) 0   B) 0.1   C) 1   D) 10

21.

22. In a recipe, the ratio of eggs to sugar is 2 eggs per 25 g of sugar. How many eggs are needed for 175 g of sugar?

A) 12   B) 13   C) 14   D) 15

22.

23. $(\frac{1}{2} \times \frac{1}{3}) \div (\frac{1}{2} - \frac{1}{3}) =$

A) $\frac{1}{6}$ B) $\frac{1}{5}$ C) $\frac{1}{2}$ D) 1

23.

24. What is the sum of the reciprocals of the four whole number factors of 6?

A) 2   B) 12   C) 1/12   D) 7/6

24.

25. $12^3 =$

A) $2^8 \times 3^3$ B) $2^6 \times 3^3$ C) $2^4 \times 3^2$ D) $2^2 \times 3^2$

25.

26. What is the product of the first four positive prime numbers?

A) 24   B) 30   C) 95   D) 210

26.

27. $\sqrt{1} + \sqrt{4} + \sqrt{9} + \sqrt{16} + \sqrt{25} + \sqrt{36} + \sqrt{49} + \sqrt{64} =$

A) 6   B) $\sqrt{6}$ C) $\sqrt{81}$ D) 6^2

27.

28. If the time now is 2:17 P.M., what will be the time 11 hours and 59 minutes from now?

A) 1:17 A.M.   B) 2:15 A.M.   C) 2:16 A.M.   D) 2:18 A.M.

28.

29. The reciprocal of the reciprocal of a number is 10. What is the number?

A) 10   B) 100   C) $\frac{1}{10}$ D) $\frac{1}{100}$

29.

30.	The ratio of boys to girls in a math class is 3:1. If 2 boys leave the class, the ratio of remaining boys to girls could *not* be A) 2:1 B) 1:1 C) 5:2 D) 1:2	30.
31.	The measure of the complement of ∠A is 30°. What is the measure of the supplement of ∠A? A) 30° B) 60° C) 120° D) 150°	31.
32.	If $\frac{2}{3}$ of a number is $\frac{1}{2}$, then the number is __?__ A) $\frac{3}{4}$ B) $\frac{1}{3}$ C) $\frac{3}{2}$ D) 3	32.
33.	If a car is traveling at 60 km per hour, how far does it travel in 72 minutes? A) 72 km B) 132 km C) 144 km D) 4320 km	33.
34.	When a certain positive number is multiplied by 2, the result is the square of the original number. The original number is A) 4 B) 3 C) 2 D) 1	34.
35.	A triangle with base 10 has the same area as a square with side 5. What is the length of the altitude to the base of the the triangle? A) 2.5 B) 5 C) 10 D) 25	35.
36.	How many whole numbers between 1 and 1991 are multiples of 5 *and* are even? A) 400 B) 399 C) 398 D) 199	36.
37.	$1\frac{1}{2} \times 1\frac{1}{3} \times 1\frac{1}{4} \times 1\frac{1}{5} \times 1\frac{1}{6} =$ A) $1\frac{1}{720}$ B) $2\frac{1}{2}$ C) 3 D) $3\frac{1}{2}$	37.
38.	$1991^2 =$ A) 2 054 081 B) 3 054 083 C) 3 964 081 D) 4 054 081	38.
39.	The measures of the angles of a quadrilateral are in the ratio 1:2:3:4. What is the measure of the smallest angle of the figure? A) 18° B) 30° C) 36° D) 72°	39.
40.	What is the ones' digit in the number 3^{1991}? A) 1 B) 3 C) 7 D) 9	40.

The end of the contest ✍ **7**

Solutions on Page 105 • Answers on Page 154

1982-83 Annual 8th Grade Contest

Tuesday, February 8, 1983

8

Instructions

- **Time** You will have only *30 minutes* working time for this contest. You might be *unable* to finish all 40 questions in the time allowed.

- **Scores** Remember *this is a contest, not a test*. There is no "passing" or "failing" score. Few students score as high as 30 points (75% correct); students with even half that, 15 points, *deserve commendation!*

- **Format and Point Value** This is a multiple-choice contest. For each question, write the *capital letter* that is *in front of* the answer you choose. For each question, your answer will be one of the *capital letters* A, B, C, or D. Each question you answer correctly is worth 1 point. Unanswered questions receive no credit.

	Answers
1. $10\,001 \times 1983 =$ A) $21\,813$ B) $200\,283$ C) $1\,984\,983$ D) $19\,831\,983$	1. D
2. $\sqrt{36} + \sqrt{64} =$ A) $\sqrt{10}$ B) $\sqrt{14}$ C) $\sqrt{100}$ D) $\sqrt{196}$	2. D
3. The ratio of the sum of the angle measures of a triangle to the sum of the angle measures of a square is A) 1:2 B) 2:3 C) 3:4 D) 4:3	3. A
4. The total number of hours in the month of February, 1983 is A) 196 B) 696 C) 672 D) 720	4. C
5. $\frac{1982}{1983} \times \frac{1983}{1984} =$ A) 1 B) $\frac{1}{2}$ C) $\frac{991}{992}$ D) $\frac{1982}{1983}$	5. B
6. 120% is the same as A) $\frac{4}{5}$ B) $\frac{5}{4}$ C) $\frac{6}{5}$ D) 120	6. C
7. The perimeter of the right triangle is A) 5 B) 6 C) 7 D) 12	7. D
8. $(-1) \times (-1) \times (-1) =$ A) -1 B) 1 C) -3 D) 3	8. A
9. Round off 87.55 to the nearest tenth. A) 90 B) 88 C) 87.5 D) 87.6	9. D
10. If x is even and a perfect square, $x < 70$, and $x > 10$, then x *could* equal A) 4 B) 25 C) 52 D) 64	10. D
11. $\frac{3}{4}$ divided by $\frac{1}{2}$ equals A) $\frac{4}{6}$ B) $\frac{3}{2}$ C) $\frac{1}{24}$ D) $\frac{3}{8}$	11. B
12. If a 3-digit whole number is multiplied by a 3-digit whole number, the product could have A) 3 digits B) 5 digits C) 7 digits D) 9 digits	12. B
13. $2^6 + 2^6 =$ A) 4^6 B) 4^{12} C) 4^{36} D) 2^7	13. D
14. The smallest one-digit prime is multiplied by the smallest two-digit prime. The product is A) 18 B) 22 C) 26 D) 33	14. B
15. Which is least? A) -1000 B) 1/100 C) 0 D) 1/1000	15. A

In question 7, the right triangle has legs labeled 3 and 4.

16. $\frac{1}{4} - \frac{1}{2} =$ A) $\frac{1}{2}$ B) $\frac{1}{4}$ C) $-\frac{1}{2}$ D) $-\frac{1}{4}$	16. D
17. One liter of syrup is mixed with four liters of water. What percent of the final mixture is syrup? B A) 25% B) 20% C) $\frac{1}{4}$% D) $\frac{1}{5}$%	17. A
18. In the rectangle, find the area of the shaded triangle. A) 16 B) 24 C) 32 D) 64	18. A
19. $3^2 + 4^2 + 12^2 =$ A) 13^2 B) 15^2 C) 17^2 D) 19^2	19. A
20. A man has 99¢ in change. If he has the fewest possible coins, how many nickels does he have? A) 0 B) 1 C) 2 D) 3	20. A
21. $\frac{2}{0.5} + \frac{5}{0.2} =$ A) 29 B) $2\frac{1}{2}$ C) 1 D) $\frac{7}{10}$	21. A
22. Which is nearest in value to $\frac{-1}{100}$? B A) -0.10 B) 0.01 C) -0.04 D) 0.10	22. C
23. Find the area of the rectangle if the radius of each circle is 4. A) 48 B) 96 C) 192 D) 384	23. D
24. $\frac{1}{12}$ is what percent of $\frac{1}{3}$? A) $\frac{1}{4}$% B) 25% C) 75% D) 400%	24. B
25. Event *A* occurs every 4 days, event *B* occurs every 6 days, and event *C* occurs every 8 days. If all three events occur on July 1, the next day that they will all occur together is A) July 9 B) July 19 C) July 24 D) July 25	25. D
26. The supplement of the complement of 60° is D A) 30° B) 60° C) 90° D) 150°	26. A
27. The average of five consecutive even numbers is 50. The smallest of these numbers is A) 42 B) 44 C) 46 D) 48	27. C
28. The average of $\frac{2}{3}$ and $\frac{5}{6}$ is A) $\frac{7}{36}$ B) $\frac{3}{4}$ C) $\frac{4}{3}$ D) $\frac{7}{18}$	28. B

Go on to the next page ⫸ **8**

29.	A room is one-half full of people. After 20 people leave, the room is one-third full. When full, the room holds A) 60 people B) 80 people C) 90 people D) 120 people	29. D
30.	Find the value of $\sqrt{8+\sqrt{64}}$. A) 4 B) 8 C) 16 D) 64	30. A
31.	If 14 *whosits* equals 35 *whatsits*, then 50 *whatsits* equals A) 125 *whosits* B) 70 *whosits* C) 20 *whosits* D) 7 *whosits*	31. C
32.	The sum of the first n positive whole numbers is $\frac{n(n+1)}{2}$. Find the sum of the first 50 positive whole numbers. A) 25×51 B) 50×51 C) 25×50 D) 50×50	32. A
33.	Find the missing number: $\frac{1}{8} + \frac{3}{8} = \frac{1}{7} + \frac{?}{7}$ A) 3 B) 4 C) $2\frac{1}{2}$ D) $3\frac{1}{2}$	33. C
34.	A baseball team has won 50 games out of 75 played. It has 45 games still to play. How many of these must the team win to give it a 60% win record for the season? A) 20 games B) 27 games C) 22 games D) 30 games	34. L
35.	In the pattern of unit squares shown in the diagram, the shaded area is A) 2 sq. units B) 3 sq. units C) 5 sq. units D) 6 sq. units	35. B
36.	The sum of the reciprocals of $x, y,$ and z most nearly equals A) −3.6 B) 0.2 C) 1 D) 1.8	36. D
37.	The hundreds' digit of $\sqrt{999\,999}$ is A) 3 B) 5 C) 7 D) 9	37. D
38.	The three touching circles shown are identical. Line segment AE is 42 units long. How long is the curved path ABCDE? A) 14π B) 21π C) 28π D) 42π	38. B
39.	A pilot flew 80 km. He flew the first 4 minutes at half speed and the second 4 minutes at full speed. The full speed of the plane is A) 400 km/hr B) 600 km/hr C) 800 km/hr D) 1000 km/hr	39. C
40.	After being painted, a solid wooden cube whose edge is 3 cm. is cut into 27 small 1-cm cubes. How many of these small cubes have exactly two painted faces? A) 18 B) 12 C) 9 D) 8	40. D

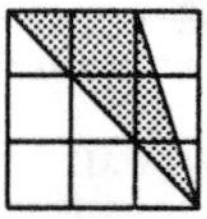

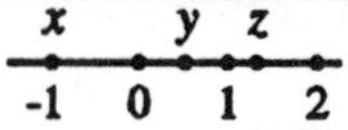

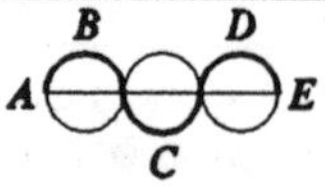

The end of the contest ✍ **8**

Solutions on Page 109 • Answers on Page 155

40

1983-84 Annual 8th Grade Contest

Tuesday, February 14, 1984

8

Instructions

- **Time** You will have only *30 minutes* working time for this contest. You might be *unable* to finish all 40 questions in the time allowed.

- **Scores** Remember *this is a contest, not a test.* There is no "passing" or "failing" score. Few students score as high as 30 points (75% correct); students with even half that, 15 points, *deserve commendation!*

- **Format and Point Value** This is a multiple-choice contest. For each question, write the *capital letter* that is *in front of* the answer you choose. For each question, your answer will be one of the *capital letters* A, B, C, or D. Each question you answer correctly is worth 1 point. Unanswered questions receive no credit.

Repeat, please bring your brain.

1. $\dfrac{1984 \times 1984}{1984} =$

   A) 1   B) 2   C) 4   D) 1984

    1. D

2. $333^2 =$

   A) 666   B) 999   C) 110 889   D) 333 333

    2. C

3. Which one of the following is a quadrilateral?

   A) rhombus   B) pentagon   C) hexagon   D) sphere

    3. A

4. $4\frac{3}{4} - 3\frac{7}{8} =$

   A) $1\frac{1}{2}$ B) $1\frac{3}{4}$ C) $1\frac{7}{8}$ D) $\frac{7}{8}$

    4. D

5. $(0.3)(0.3) =$

   A) $\frac{1}{3}$ B) $\frac{3}{100}$ C) $\frac{90}{100}$ D) $\frac{9}{100}$

    5. D

6. $\dfrac{1-2}{2-1} =$

   A) 1   B) $\frac{1}{2}$ C) 0   D) –1

    6. D

7. The largest prime factor of 77 000 000 is

   A) 3   B) 5   C) 7   D) 11

    7. D

8. $(\frac{4}{3} + \frac{10}{9} + \frac{28}{27}) - (\frac{1}{3} + \frac{1}{9} + \frac{1}{27}) =$

   A) 0   B) 1   C) 2   D) 3

    8. D

9. Which is the greatest common divisor of 1984 and 1986?

   A) 1   B) 2   C) 4   D) 8

    9. B

10. $0.888 + 0.222 =$

   A) 1.000   B) 1.010   C) 1.110   D) 1.111

    10. C

11. The measure of one angle of an isosceles triangle is 120°. The measures of each of the other angles is

   A) 30°   B) 40°   C) 60°   D) 120°

    11. A

12. Which number is equal to its own reciprocal?

   A) 0   B) $\frac{1}{2}$ C) $\frac{2}{3}$ D) 1

    12. D

13. $\dfrac{5 \times 10 \times 15 \times 20}{5 \times 5 \times 5 \times 5} =$

   A) 10   B) 12   C) 24   D) 750

    13. C

14. (10% of 20) minus (20% of 10) =

   A) 2   B) $\frac{1}{2}$ C) 1   D) 0

    14. D

15. The product of two whole numbers is 36. Their greatest possible sum is

   A) 12   B) 13   C) 20   D) 37

    15. D

Go on to the next page ▮▮▮➡ **8**

16. The sum of two whole numbers is 36. Their greatest possible product is
    A) 35   B) 260   C) 320   D) 324

16. D

17. $62\frac{1}{2}\% =$
    A) $\frac{3}{5}$ B) $\frac{5}{8}$ C) $\frac{5}{6}$ D) $\frac{2}{3}$

17. B

18. On segment $\overline{AC}$, $AB = 8$ and $AB:BC = 2:5$. Find AC.

    A   B   C

    A) 20   B) 24   C) 28   D) 40

18. C

19. The sum of the digits of a five-digit number can never equal
    A) 1   B) 37   C) 44   D) 50

19. D

20. The average of $\frac{1}{5}$ and $\frac{1}{7}$ is
    A) $\frac{12}{35}$ B) $\frac{1}{6}$ C) $\frac{1}{12}$ D) $\frac{6}{35}$

20. D

21. The perimeter of a rectangle is $\frac{1}{9}$. The sum of the lengths of two adjacent sides is
    A) $\frac{1}{36}$ B) $\frac{1}{18}$ C) $\frac{2}{3}$ D) $\frac{2}{9}$

21. B

22. Find the missing number: 125% of 16 = 20% of _?_
    A) 20   B) 80   C) 100   D) 120

22. C

23. The fewest number of sides which a polygon can have is
    A) 2   B) 3   C) 4   D) 5

23. B

24. If 75% of a number is 36, then 150% of the number is
    A) 18   B) 48   C) 54   D) 72

24. D

25. $\dfrac{1 - \frac{1}{2}}{1 + \frac{1}{2}} =$

    A) 6   B) 3   C) $\frac{1}{2}$ D) $\frac{1}{3}$

25. D

26. Equilateral triangle ABC rests atop square $ACDE$. The measure of angle BCD is

    B

    A   C
    E   D

    A) 30°   B) 60°   C) 90°   D) 150°

26. D

27. On an $800 loan (at a 12% annual interest rate), the simple interest for 9 months is
    A) $24   B) $48   C) $72   D) $96

27. C

28. A sailboat sails 6 km south and then 8 km east. At that moment, how far is the sailboat from its starting point?
    A) 10 km   B) 12 km   C) 14 km   D) 48 km

28. A

Go on to the next page ▐▐▶ **8**

29.	A certain soap is $99\frac{44}{100}\%$ pure. The percent of impurities is A) $\frac{16}{25}\%$ B) $\frac{33}{50}\%$ C) $\frac{14}{25}\%$ D) $1\frac{44}{100}\%$	29. C
30.	What is the difference between the area of a rectangle 10 m by 6 m and the area of a square having the same perimeter? A) 165 sq. m B) 56 sq. m C) 8 sq. m D) 4 sq. m	30. D
31.	A train travels 24 km in 36 minutes. Its rate of speed, in km per hour, is A) 60 B) 48 C) 45 D) 40	31. D
32.	The average of all the whole numbers from 1 to 100 is A) 49 B) $49\frac{1}{2}$ C) 50 D) $50\frac{1}{2}$	32. D
33.	Which choice is the average of the other three choices? A) 2^5 B) 3^3 C) 5^2 D) $2^2 \times 7$	33. D
34.	If $a \blacklozenge b$ means $(a \times b) + b$, then $2 \blacklozenge 3$ has the value A) 12 B) 9 C) 8 D) 6	34. B
35.	A whole number is called an *increasing number* if each digit in the number is greater then the digit to its left. For example, 2359 is an increasing number. How many increasing numbers are there between 5000 and 10000? A) 3 B) 4 C) 5 D) 6	35. C
36.	If $3x = 21$, then $21x =$ A) 3 B) 7 C) 63 D) 147	36. D
37.	How many different three-digit numbers can be made using any three of the following five digits: 1, 2, 2, 3, and 3? A) 12 B) 16 C) 18 D) 20	37. C
38.	In which are the fractions $\frac{2}{3}, \frac{3}{4}, \frac{5}{8},$ and $\frac{5}{7}$ arranged in decreasing order, from left to right? A) $\frac{5}{8}, \frac{5}{7}, \frac{3}{4}, \frac{2}{3}$ B) $\frac{5}{7}, \frac{3}{4}, \frac{2}{3}, \frac{5}{8}$ C) $\frac{3}{4}, \frac{5}{7}, \frac{2}{3}, \frac{5}{8}$ D) $\frac{2}{3}, \frac{5}{7}, \frac{3}{4}, \frac{5}{8}$	38. C
39.	An ant crawls outside a square of side 1 cm, at all times remaining exactly 1 cm from the boundary of the square. In square cm, the area bounded by one complete circuit of the ant is most nearly equal to A) 7 B) 8 C) 9 D) 10	39. B
40.	What is the missing length in the diagram (which is not drawn to scale)? A) 12 B) 15 C) 18 D) 21	40. C

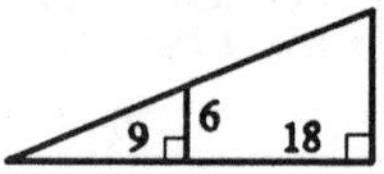

The end of the contest ✍ **8**

Solutions on Page 113 • Answers on Page 156

44

1984-85 Annual 8th Grade Contest
Tuesday, February 12, 1985

8

Instructions

■ **Time** You will have only *30 minutes* working time for this contest. You might be *unable* to finish all 40 questions in the time allowed.

■ **Scores** Remember *this is a contest, not a test.* There is no "passing" or "failing" score. Few students score as high as 30 points (75% correct); students with even half that, 15 points, *deserve commendation!*

■ **Format and Point Value** This is a multiple-choice contest. For each question, write the *capital letter* that is *in front of* the answer you choose. For each question, your answer will be one of the *capital letters* A, B, C, or D. Each question you answer correctly is worth 1 point. Unanswered questions receive no credit.

Copyright © 1985 by Mathematics Leagues Inc.

Answers

1. 1985 divided by 1984 =
   A) $\frac{1}{1984}$ B) $\frac{1984}{1985}$ C) 1   D) $1\frac{1}{1984}$

1. D

2. One hundred times π is most nearly equal to
   A) 300   B) 314   C) 315   D) 316

2. D

3. 1234 + 2143 + 3412 + 4321 =
   A) 1110   B) 11110   C) 10010   D) 11010

3. B

4. Mickey Mouse is requested to file 800 cards. If he can file cards at the rate of 80 cards an hour, the number of cards remaining to be filed after 7 hours of work is
   A) 560   B) 140   C) 240   D) 260

4. D

5. Seventeen thousandths =
   A) 17 000   B) 0.170   C) 0.017   D) 0.0017

5. D

6. The number of tens in 1000 is
   A) 3   B) 10   C) 100   D) 1000

6. C

7. $\sqrt{144} \times \sqrt{400}$ =
   A) 240   B) 256   C) 576   D) 14400

7. A

8. Which of the following is *not* a quadrilateral?
   A) square   B) trapezoid   C) pentagon   D) rhombus

8. C

9. 18 − _?_ = 20
   A) −2   B) −38   C) 2   D) 38

9. A

10. How many numbers between 1 and 100 are equal to 6 times an integer?
    A) 6   B) 16   C) 17   D) 96

10. B

11. Which of the following is *not* equal to $12\frac{1}{2}$%?
    A) 12.5   B) 0.125   C) 12.5%   D) $\frac{1}{8}$

11. A

12. $\frac{3}{2} + \frac{5}{4} + \frac{9}{8} + \frac{17}{16} - 4$ =
    A) $\frac{1}{16}$ B) $\frac{1}{4}$ C) $\frac{1}{2}$ D) $\frac{15}{16}$

12. D

13. Which is greater than $\frac{1}{2}$?
    A) $\frac{4}{9}$ B) $\frac{5}{11}$ C) $\frac{6}{12}$ D) $\frac{7}{13}$

13. D

14. 0.0125 =
    A) $\frac{125}{1000}$ B) $\frac{1}{8}$ C) $\frac{1}{80}$ D) $\frac{12.5}{10000}$

14. C

15. A square and an equilateral triangle have equal perimeters. The perimeter of the triangle is 12. Find the area of the square.
    A) 9   B) 16   C) 36   D) 81

15. A

16. 49 divided by 0.035 =
    A) 1.4   B) 14   C) 140   D) 1400

16. D

17. The number of prime numbers between 45 and 65 is

    A) 3   B) 4   C) 5   D) 6

    17. B

18. If, in the figure, $\overline{PQ}$ and $\overline{RS}$ are intersecting line segments, $x + y =$

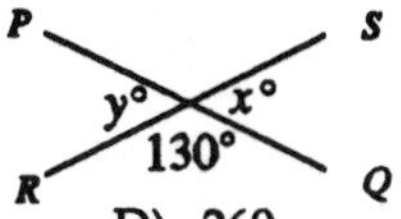

    A) 50   B) 100   C) 180   D) 260

    18. B

19. $\dfrac{8 \times 9 \times 10}{9 \times 10} \times \dfrac{6 \times 7}{6 \times 7 \times 8} =$

    A) 1   B) 0   C) $\frac{1}{64}$ D) 65

    19. A

20. If the circumference of a circle is divided by the length of its radius, the result is

    A) 1   B) π C) 2   D) 2π

    20. D

21. $(-6) - (-7) + (-8) - (9) =$

    A) −30   B) −16   C) 0   D) 2

    21. B

22. The area of a triangle is 16. The length of one side is 8. The length of the altitude to this side is

    A) 1   B) 2   C) 4   D) 8

    22. C

23. $\dfrac{4\frac{1}{3}}{4} = \dfrac{?}{12}$

    A) 26   B) 13   C) 8   D) 7

    23. B

24. Which of the following sets of numbers could represent the lengths of the sides of a right triangle?

    A) 9, 16, 25   B) 1, 2, 3   C) 1, $\sqrt{2}$, $\sqrt{3}$ D) 5, 15, 17

    24. C

25. If 2 is divided by $\frac{1}{2}$, the result is

    A) 1   B) $\frac{1}{4}$ C) 2   D) 4

    25. D

26. How many whole numbers between 700 and 900 begin and/or end with an 8.

    A) 100   B) 110   C) 120   D) 140

    26. B

27. If $\frac{3}{4}$ of a number is 48, then $\frac{3}{16}$ of the number is

    A) 12   B) 18   C) 24   D) 192

    27. A

28. If each side of a square is decreased 10%, then the area of the square is decreased

    A) 40%   B) 20%   C) 19%   D) 10%

    28. C

29. If $1\frac{1}{3}$ is subtracted from its reciprocal, the result is

    A) $\frac{7}{12}$ B) 0   C) $-\frac{1}{12}$ D) $-\frac{7}{12}$

    29. D

30. The distance from P to Q is

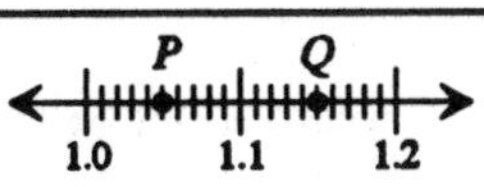

    A) 0.05   B) 0.10   C) 0.50   D) 1.00

    30. B

31. Marina types 5 pages in 4 minutes. Ruth types 1 page in 1 minute. In 7 hours, how many more pages will Marina type than Ruth?
A) 105   B) 84   C) 15   D) 140

31. A

32. If half as many people lived in Toronto as lived in the rest of Ontario, what percent of Ontario's residents would live in Toronto
A) $33\frac{1}{3}\%$ B) 25%   C) 20%   D) 50%

32. A

33. The 1985th positive odd number is
A) 1985   B) 1987   C) 3969   D) 3971

33. C

34. If 10% of a number is 2 less than 20% of the same number, then 80% of the number equals
A) 4   B) 8   C) 16   D) 32

34. C

35. Five cars (each of the same length) plus eight trucks (each of the same length) take up the same room in a warehouse as 11 trucks. How many cars can fit into a warehouse which can hold 30 trucks?
A) 18   B) 30   C) 50   D) 80

35. C

36. $2^8 \times 5^6 =$
A) 4 555 555   B) 2 560 000   C) 4 000 000   D) 5 400 400

36. C

37. What fraction of the integral multiples of 3, between 1 and 100, are also integral multiples of 4?
A) $\frac{1}{4}$ B) $\frac{8}{33}$ C) $\frac{25}{33}$ D) $\frac{1}{12}$

37. B

38. Suppose $a*b = \frac{a+b}{a \times b}$ for any two positive numbers a and b. Then, $3*4 = \frac{3+4}{3 \times 4} = \frac{7}{12}$. What does $(3*4)*5$ equal?
A) $\frac{35}{12}$ B) $\frac{67}{420}$ C) $\frac{1}{35}$ D) $\frac{67}{35}$

38. D

39. Which of the following figures can *not* be folded along the dotted lines to form a cube?
A) 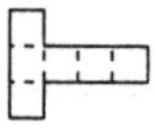   B) 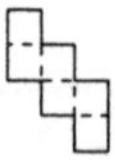   C) 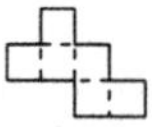   D)

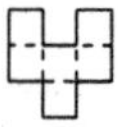

39. D

40. The 1985th digit to the right of the decimal point in the decimal expansion of $\frac{1}{7}$ is
A) 2   B) 4   C) 5   D) 8

40. C

The end of the contest   8

Solutions on Page 117 • Answers on Page 157

48

MATH LEAGUE PRESS

P.O. BOX 720, TENAFLY, NEW JERSEY 07670

1985-86 Annual 8th Grade Contest

Tuesday, February 11, 1986

8

Instructions

- **Time** You will have only *30 minutes* working time for this contest. You might be *unable* to finish all 40 questions in the time allowed.

- **Scores** Remember *this is a contest, not a test.* There is no "passing" or "failing" score. Few students score as high as 30 points (75% correct); students with even half that, 15 points, *deserve commendation!*

- **Format and Point Value** This is a multiple-choice contest. For each question, write the *capital letter* that is *in front of* the answer you choose. For each question, your answer will be one of the *capital letters* A, B, C, or D. Each question you answer correctly is worth 1 point. Unanswered questions receive no credit.

	Answers
1. $\frac{1}{10} + \frac{2}{10} + \frac{3}{10} + \frac{4}{10} =$ A) $\frac{1}{4}$ B) $\frac{11}{10}$ C) $\frac{7}{30}$ D) 1	1. D
2. Carol bought 10 pens at 89¢ per pen. She paid for the pens with a $10 bill. How much change did she receive? A) $1.10 B) 79¢ C) $9.11 D) $2.10	2. A
3. $0.77 + 0.7 =$ A) 0.84 B) 1.47 C) 0.777 D) 7.77	3. B
4. The sum of the measures of any *two* angles of an equilateral triangle is always A) 60° B) 90° C) 120° D) 180°	4. C
5. $\frac{21}{56} =$ A) 0.37 B) $\frac{3}{4}$ C) $37\frac{1}{2}\%$ D) $\frac{3}{7}$	5. C
6. $45.2 - 35.3 =$ A) 9.9 B) 10.9 C) 10.1 D) 9.1	6. A
7. If today is Tuesday, what day will it be 777 days from today? A) Monday B) Tuesday C) Wednesday D) Thursday	7. B
8. $3\frac{5}{6} + \frac{2}{3} =$ A) $4\frac{1}{2}$ B) $4\frac{1}{3}$ C) $4\frac{2}{3}$ D) $3\frac{7}{9}$	8. A
9. $0.2 \times 0.2 =$ A) 4 B) $\frac{1}{4}$ C) 0.4 D) 0.04	9. D
10. Find the missing number: $\sqrt{25} \times \sqrt{25} = 25 \times$ __?__ A) 1 B) 5 C) 10 D) 25	10. A
11. Which is equal to one-fifth of one-fifth? A) $\frac{1}{25}$ B) $\frac{1}{10}$ C) $\frac{1}{5}$ D) $\frac{1}{2}$	11. A
12. Which one of the following *could* be the measure of one of the angles of a right triangle? A) 89° B) 91° C) 93° D) 95°	12. A
13. When a pole 30 m tall casts a shadow 15 m long, what would be the length of the shadow cast by a 150 m pole? A) 3 m B) 30 m C) 75 m D) 135 m	13. C
14. $(-1) \times (-2) \times (-3) \times (-4) =$ A) -24 B) -10 C) 24 D) 10	14. C
15. Which of the following most nearly equals 49.5 divided by 0.5? A) 10 B) 25 C) 50 D) 100	15. D

Go on to the next page ⁍ **8**

16. $(1 - \frac{1}{2}) + (\frac{1}{2} - \frac{1}{3}) + (\frac{1}{3} - \frac{1}{4}) =$ A) 1 B) $1\frac{1}{2}$ C) $\frac{3}{4}$ D) $\frac{1}{4}$	16. C
17. $2^6 - 2^5 =$ A) 1 B) 2^1 C) 2^4 D) 2^5	17. D
18. The area of square I is 4. The perimeter of square II is three times the perimeter of square I. The area of square II is A) 12 B) 36 C) 48 D) 144	18. B
19. $\frac{2.4}{5} =$ A) $\frac{12}{5}$ B) $\frac{12}{25}$ C) $\frac{6}{125}$ D) $\frac{12}{125}$	19. B
20. If 3 times a number is $10\frac{1}{2}$, the number is A) $3\frac{1}{2}$ B) $4\frac{1}{2}$ C) $16\frac{1}{2}$ D) $31\frac{1}{2}$	20. A
21. In the diagram at the right, if $m\angle e + m\angle f = 150°$ and $m\angle g + m\angle a + m\angle b + m\angle d = 190°$, find $m\angle c$. A) 20° B) 40° C) 50° D) 340°	21. A
22. If one-half of a number is 24, then twice the number must be A) 12 B) 24 C) 48 D) 96	22. D
23. Round 0.999 to the nearest tenth. A) 0.1 B) 0.9 C) 0.99 D) 1.0	23. D
24. The sum of two numbers is 11. The product of the two numbers is 24. The larger of the two numbers is A) 4 B) 6 C) 8 D) 12	24. C
25. The average of three numbers is 25. If two of the numbers are 20 and 30, the third number is A) 0 B) 20 C) 25 D) 30	25. C
26. Which of the following is largest? A) 0.125 B) $\frac{3}{24}$ C) 125% D) $\frac{1\frac{1}{2}}{12}$	26. C
27. Which of the following is most nearly equal to 1? A) $\frac{99}{100}$ B) $1\frac{1}{99}$ C) 0.9 D) 1.1	27. A
28. If $5 < x < 9$ and $0 < y < 4$, which is *always* true? A) $x < y$ B) $x + y > xy$ C) $xy > 50$ D) $x > y$	28. D
29. $2^7 \times 5^6 =$ A) 2 555 555 B) 1 280 000 C) 2 000 000 D) 5 200 200	29. C

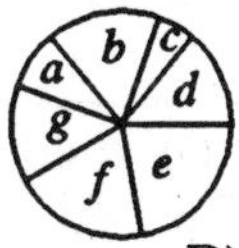

30. In the diagram at the right, the length of a diameter of the circle is 2 and the length of a side of the square is 3. The area of the shaded region is A) 5　　　B) 9−π　　　C) 9−2π　　　D) 9−4π	30. *B*
31. If ■ × ■ + ▼ = ▼, then ■ = A) −1　　　B) 0　　　C) $\frac{1}{2}$　　　D) 1	31. *B*
32. If each side of a square is increased by 50%, the area of the square is increased by A) 50%　　B) 100%　　C) 125%　　D) 225%	32. *C*
33. A circular pizza of radius 8 is cut into 8 equal slices. The perimeter of one slice is A) 16+2π　　B) 2π　　C) 8π　　D) 8+4π	33. *A*
34. The smallest possible number of Mondays that can occur during a period of 45 consecutive days is A) 5　　　B) 6　　　C) 7　　　D) 9	34. *B*
35. Five minutes after my English class was half over, one-third of the class period remained. My English class takes a total of A) 15 minutes B) 20 minutes C) 24 minutes D) 30 minutes	35. *D*
36. How many pairs of parallel edges does a rectangular solid have? A) 8　　　B) 12　　　C) 16　　　D) 18	36. *D*
37. The difference between two prime numbers is 1985. The larger of these two prime numbers is A) 2431　　B) 2002　　C) 1987　　D) 1986	37. *C*
38. The symbol *n*! means the product of all the natural numbers from 1 through *n*. For example, 4! = 4×3×2×1 = 24. The units' digit of 11! + 10! + 9! + 8! + 7! + 6! + 5! + 4! + 3! + 2! is A) 0　　　B) 1　　　C) 2　　　D) 3	38. *C*
39. A sequence of numbers is called a *Fibonacci-type Sequence* if each number (after for the first two) is the sum of the two numbers which precede it. For example, 1, 1, 2, 3, 5, 8, . . . is a *Fibonacci-type Sequence*. If 1985, *x*, *y*, 2000 are four consecutive terms in a *Fibonacci-type Sequence*, then *x* equals A) 1990　　B) 1995　　C) 1999　　D) $7\frac{1}{2}$	39. *D*
40. The number of seconds in 2 hours equals the number of minutes in A) 1 day　　B) 2 days　　C) 4 days　　D) 5 days	40. *D*

The end of the contest ✍ **8**

Solutions on Page 121 • Answers on Page 158

1986-87 Annual 8th Grade Contest

Tuesday, February 10, 1987

8

Instructions

- **Time** You will have only *30 minutes* working time for this contest. You might be *unable* to finish all 40 questions in the time allowed.

- **Scores** Remember *this is a contest, not a test.* There is no "passing" or "failing" score. Few students score as high as 30 points (75% correct); students with even half that, 15 points, *deserve commendation!*

- **Format and Point Value** This is a multiple-choice contest. For each question, write the *capital letter* that is *in front of* the answer you choose. For each question, your answer will be one of the *capital letters* A, B, C, or D. Each question you answer correctly is worth 1 point. Unanswered questions receive no credit.

1.	Which one of the following is an *even* number? A) 198^7 B) 19×87 C) 19^{87} D) $1+9+87$	1. A
2.	100% of 50 = A) 5000 B) 500 C) 50 D) 0.5	2. C
3.	Each of the following is equal to $\frac{2}{5}$ *except* A) $\frac{4}{10}$ B) $\frac{22}{55}$ C) 40% D) 0.04	3. D
4.	The product of two whole numbers is 100. What is the *largest* possible *sum* of these two numbers? A) 101 B) 52 C) 29 D) 20	4. A
5.	$\frac{5}{6} \times \frac{6}{7} \times \frac{7}{8} \times \frac{8}{9} =$ A) $\frac{1}{9}$ B) 1 C) $\frac{9}{5}$ D) $\frac{5}{9}$	5. D
6.	$\sqrt{25^2}$ A) 5 B) 25 C) 312.5 D) 625	6. B
7.	19 meters + 87 centimeters = A) 0.1987 cm B) 19.87 cm C) 198.7 cm D) 1987 cm	7. D
8.	$\frac{\pi}{2} - \frac{\pi}{3} =$ A) $\frac{1}{6}$ B) $\frac{\pi}{6}$ C) $\frac{2\pi}{6}$ D) $\frac{5\pi}{6}$	8. B
9.	Of the following, which is the largest number? A) $\frac{100}{199}$ B) $\frac{1}{2}$ C) $\frac{49}{99}$ D) $\frac{98}{197}$	9. A
10.	$\frac{0.77}{2} =$ A) 0.385 B) 1.54 C) 3.85 D) 38.5	10. A
11.	Which of the following is a prime number? A) 1985 B) 1986 C) 1987 D) 1988	11. C
12.	A bell rings every 2 seconds, and a bird chirps every 3 seconds. If the ring and the chirp occur together right now, they will also occur together in A) 40 seconds B) 41 seconds C) 42 seconds D) 43 seconds	12. C
13.	Find the missing number: (5% of 40) + (15% of 40) = (_?_ of 80). A) 5% B) 10% C) 20% D) 40%	13. D
14.	If ray *BD* bisects right angle *ABC*, the measure of angle *ABD* is A) 180° B) 90° C) 50° D) 45°	14. B
15.	If *A* is 25% more than *B*, then *B* is _?_ less than *A*. A) 10% B) 15% C) 20% D) 25%	15. C

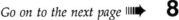

Go on to the next page ⟶ **8**

#	Question	Answer
16.	The product of 3, 4, and 5 equals the sum of 4×5 and A) 3 B) 3×5 C) 8 D) 8×5	16. D
17.	Find the missing number: $\frac{1}{4} \times \frac{1}{4} \times \frac{1}{4} = 4 \times 4 \times \underline{\ ?\ }$ A) $\frac{1}{1024}$ B) $\frac{1}{64}$ C) $\frac{1}{4}$ D) 4	17. A
18.	10 seconds is what fractional part of 10 hours? A) $\frac{1}{60}$ B) $\frac{1}{360}$ C) $\frac{1}{3600}$ D) $\frac{1}{36000}$	18. C
19.	When 0.48 is divided by 0.016, the quotient is A) 300 B) 30 C) 3 D) 0.3	19. B
20.	Of the following, which is the smallest? A) 0.05 B) $\frac{1}{5}$ C) $\frac{1}{2}\%$ D) 0.1	20. C
21.	What is the fewest number of 7's that can be added together to make their sum greater than 4000? A) 4001 B) 572 C) 571 D) 470	21. B
22.	Dan had $2\frac{1}{2}$ cookies and ate $\frac{1}{2}$ of a cookie. Of the *original* number of cookies, the fractional part that he ate was A) $\frac{1}{2}$ B) $\frac{1}{4}$ C) $\frac{1}{5}$ D) $\frac{1}{8}$	22. C
23.	The average of 3 numbers is between 7 and 10. The sum of the numbers could be any of the following *except* A) 20 B) 22 C) 26 D) 28	23. A
24.	If three-quarters of a number is 24, the number itself must be A) 32 B) 30 C) 18 D) 16	24. A
25.	On a scale drawing, 2 centimeters represent 50 meters. How many centimeters represent 5 meters? A) 10 B) 0.02 C) 0.2 D) $\frac{1}{10}$	25. C
26.	If 2 is added to a number, and the result is then multiplied by 3, the final result is 25. The original number was most nearly A) 11 B) 10 C) 7 D) 6	26. D
27.	Find the missing number: $6^2 + 8^2 - 10^2 =$ A) 0 B) 4 C) 6 D) 12	27. A
28.	A whole number is first multiplied by 2 and then by 5. The result *could* be A) 12 B) 25 C) 50 D) 55	28. C
29.	Which number is most nearly equal to 99π? A) 310 B) 311 C) 313 D) 314	29. B

Go on to the next page ⟹ 8

55

30. How many more cartons are needed to hold 1500 books in cartons of 10 than in cartons of 15? A) 5 B) 50 C) 100 D) 500	30. B
31. The square of $\frac{1}{4}$ equals the square root of A) $\frac{1}{2}$ B) $\frac{1}{4}$ C) $\frac{1}{16}$ D) $\frac{1}{256}$	31. D
32. When the perimeter of an equilateral triangle is doubled, the result is 24. The length of a side of the original triangle is A) 4 B) 6 C) 8 D) 12	32. A
33. Al is twice as old as Bill, who is twice as old as Carl. In 10 years, Al will be twice as old as Carl. How old is Al now? A) 40 B) 20 C) 10 D) 5	33. B
34. If B is the midpoint of $\overline{AC}$, and if C is the midpoint of $\overline{BD}$, then what percent of CD is AC? A) 25% B) 50% C) 100% D) 200%	34. D
35. If b books cost d dollars, then d books cost A) b dollars B) bd dollars C) $\frac{d^2}{b}$ dollars D) $\frac{b^2}{d}$ dollars	35. C
36. A wheel with a diameter of 2 meters rolls on the street for 100 meters. Most nearly, the wheel made ? complete revolutions. A) 64 B) 32 C) 16 D) 8	36. C
37. The volume of cube I is 331 m³ less than the volume if cube II. If an edge of cube I is 10 meters, an edge of cube II is A) 14 meters B) 13 meters C) 12 meters D) 11 meters	37. D
38. Action Comic #1, which originally sold for 10¢, now sells for $18500. This comic has increased in value A) 18500000% B) 185000% C) 1849990% D) 18499900%	38.
39. Trains A and B, 200 km apart on the same straight track, travel at speeds of 50 km/hr and 65 km/hr respectively. At the end of 1 hour, the distance between the trains could *not* be A) 85 km B) 115 km C) 185 km D) 215 km	39. B
40. To form a certain sequence, the rules are: ■ if a number is even, divide by 2 to get the next number; ■ if a number is odd, multiply by 3, then add 1 to get the next number. Starting with 12, the first few terms are 12, 6, 3, 10, 5, 16, ... In *this* particular sequence, the 1000th term is A) 1 B) 2 C) 3 D) 4	40.

The end of the contest 🖎 **8**

Solutions on Page 125 • Answers on Page 159

1987-88 Annual 8th Grade Contest

Tuesday, February 2, 1988

8

Instructions

- **Time** You will have only *30 minutes* working time for this contest. You might be *unable* to finish all 40 questions in the time allowed.

- **Scores** Remember *this is a contest, not a test.* There is no "passing" or "failing" score. Few students score as high as 30 points (75% correct); students with even half that, 15 points, *deserve commendation!*

- **Format and Point Value** This is a multiple-choice contest. For each question, write the *capital letter* that is *in front of* the answer you choose. For each question, your answer will be one of the *capital letters* A, B, C, or D. Each question you answer correctly is worth 1 point. Unanswered questions receive no credit.

		Answers
1.	The value of 7 quarters, 6 dimes, 5 nickels, and 4 pennies is A) 22¢ B) $1.64 C) $2.64 D) $3.64	1. C
2.	$1988 - \frac{1985}{1988} =$ A) $1987\frac{3}{1988}$ B) $1987\frac{1985}{1988}$ C) $1988\frac{3}{1988}$ D) $1988\frac{1985}{1988}$	2. A
3.	$10 - 9 + 8 - 7 + 6 - 5 + 4 - 3 + 2 - 1 =$ A) 9 B) 5 C) 3 D) 1	3. B
4.	The product of two whole numbers is 100. One of the numbers is 48 more than the other. The larger of the two numbers is A) 2 B) 48 C) 50 D) 96	4. C
5.	$\frac{19}{88} \times \frac{88}{19} =$ A) 1 B) $\frac{1988}{8819}$ C) $\frac{19}{88}$ D) 0	5. A
6.	In triangle ABC, angle C is a 60° angle. If $AC = BC = 5$, then the measure of angle B is A) 60° B) 45° C) 30° D) 12°	6. A
7.	$\sqrt{16 \times 16} =$ A) 2 B) 4 C) 8 D) 16	7. D
8.	Which of the following is greater than $-\frac{5}{2}$? A) $-\frac{8}{3}$ B) $-\frac{7}{3}$ C) $-\frac{7}{2}$ D) -3	8. B
9.	A rectangular lot measures 42 m by 26 m. If I walk around the boundary of this lot once, I'll have walked a total distance of A) 68 m B) 104 m C) 136 m D) 272 m	9. C
10.	When $\frac{2}{3}$ is divided by $\frac{3}{2}$, the quotient is A) 1 B) $\frac{4}{9}$ C) $\frac{9}{4}$ D) 0	10. B
11.	$0.19 + 0.88 =$ A) 0.1988 B) 0.278 C) 0.97 D) 1.07	11. D
12.	After Sandy received a 50% increase in salary, Sandy then made $300 per week. Previously, Sandy's weekly salary was A) $150 B) $200 C) $250 D) $275	12. B
13.	In the diagram, the perimeter of the larger square is 20 and the perimeter of the smaller square is 16. The area of the region between the two squares is A) 1 B) 2 C) 4 D) 9	13. D
14.	$0.66 =$ A) $\frac{1}{3}$ B) $\frac{2}{3}$ C) $\frac{6}{7}$ D) $\frac{33}{50}$	14. D

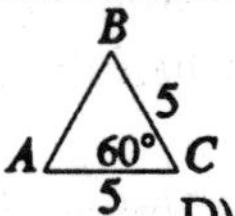

Go on to the next page ▐▌▶ **8**

15. $\frac{20\%}{100} =$

A) $\frac{1}{5}$ B) $\frac{1}{50}$ C) $\frac{1}{500}$ D) $\frac{1}{5000}$

15.

16. One hundred eighth-graders at a school had a class party. They ordered enough pizzas so that each of them could have exactly 2 slices. If each pizza has 8 slices, they ordered

A) 50 pizzas   B) 25 pizzas   C) 200 pizzas   D) 100 pizzas

16. B

17. $(-1)^{1989} - (-1)^{1988} =$

A) -2 B) -1 C) 0 D) 2

17. A

18. On a map, 2 cm represents 50 km. The distance between two towns on this map is 7.5 cm. Their actual distance apart is

A) 375 km   B) 275 km   C) 187.5 km   D) 75 km

18. C

19. $(\frac{1}{3} \times 11) + (\frac{1}{3} \times 13) =$

A) $\frac{1}{3} \times 12$ B) $\frac{1}{3} \times 24$ C) $\frac{2}{3} \times 12$ D) $\frac{2}{3} \times 24$

19. B

20. The number of vertices in a cube is

A) 4   B) 6   C) 8   D) 12

20. C

21. In the diagram, triangle *ABC* is an equilateral triangle. The sum of the measures of the angles marked 1 and 2 is

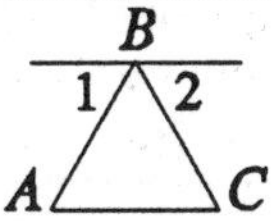

A) 60°   B) 90°   C) 120°   D) 180°

21. C

22. Which of the following numbers is smaller than its reciprocal?

A) $\frac{1987}{1988}$ B) $\frac{1988}{1987}$ C) $1\frac{1}{3}$ D) $-\frac{2}{3}$

22. A

23. The number of eighths in 5.75 is

A) 8   B) 23   C) 46   D) 120

23. C

24. Steve, who usually jogs for $2\frac{1}{2}$ hours, increased his jogging time to 3 hours. This increase over the usual time is

A) 10%   B) 20%   C) 25%   D) 50%

24. B

25. A number is multiplied by 5, then divided by 6. The result is $\frac{3}{8}$. The original number was

A) $\frac{5}{16}$ B) $\frac{5}{6}$ C) $\frac{6}{5}$ D) $\frac{9}{20}$

25. D

26. $75\% - \frac{2}{3} =$

A) $\frac{1}{12}$ B) $\frac{1}{10}$ C) $\frac{1}{9}$ D) $\frac{3}{10}$

26. A

27. The square root of the area of a square is 25. The area of the square is

A) 625   B) 100   C) 25   D) 5

27. A

28. The circumference of a circle, divided by its radius, equals

A) $\frac{\pi}{2}$ B) π C) $\frac{3\pi}{2}$ D) 2π

28. D

29. The square root of $\frac{1}{4}$ is A) $\frac{1}{2}$ B) $\frac{1}{8}$ C) $\frac{1}{16}$ D) $\frac{1}{64}$	29. A
30. The ratio of 2.5 to 7.5 is equivalent to A) 2:7 B) 7:2 C) 3:1 D) 1:3	30. D
31. One-fourth of a 520 cm log is cut off. Then $\frac{4}{5}$ of the remainder is cut off. How much of the log remains? A) 26 cm B) 78 cm C) 104 cm D) 312 cm	31. B
32. In the accompanying circle shown at the right, O is the center. In $\triangle OAB$, angles O and A have equal measures. The measure of angle B is A) 30° B) 45° C) 60° D) 180°	32. C
33. Let $\#N$ mean the number of days in year N. What is the value of $\#1988 + \#1989 + \#1990 + \#1991$? A) 1460 B) 1461 C) 1462 D) 1463	33. B
34. Two different numbers are chosen from the sequence of consecutive odd integers 51, 53, 55, . . . , 95, 97, 99. Which of the following could *not* be their sum? A) 161 B) 168 C) 186 D) 196	34. A
35. 999^2 is between A) 10^3 and 10^4 B) 10^4 and 10^5 C) 10^5 and 10^6 D) 10^6 and 10^7	35. C
36. If $x + 3$ represents an even number, then which of the following will *always* represent an odd number? A) $x + 1$ B) $6x + 4$ C) $3x + 5$ D) $5x + 8$	36. D
37. The sum of the first 1 million primes is N. Without knowing N's value, one can determine that the ones' digit of N cannot be a A) 1 B) 2 C) 3 D) 9	37. B
38. If $\frac{a}{b} = 5\%$, then $\frac{6a}{5b} =$ A) 6% B) 25% C) 30% D) $\frac{6}{5}\%$	38. A
39. Between 3 P.M. and 3:30 P.M., the minute hand of a clock moves 180°. How many degrees does the hour hand move during that same period of time? A) 2.5° B) 15° C) 20° D) 30°	39. B
40. Jack and Jill went to Burger Queen. Jack bought 2 hamburgers and 3 shakes for \$4.21 while Jill bought 3 hamburgers and 2 shakes for \$5.24. The cost of 1 hamburger and 1 shake is A) \$1.03 B) \$1.54 C) \$1.89 D) \$9.45	40.

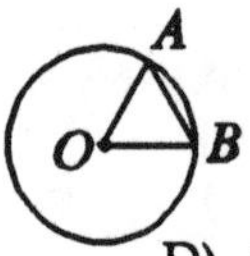

The end of the contest 🖐 **8**

Solutions on Page 129 • Answers on Page 160

MATH LEAGUE PRESS

P.O. BOX 720, TENAFLY, NEW JERSEY 07670

1988-89 Annual 8th Grade Contest

Tuesday, February 7, 1989

8

Instructions

- **Time** You will have only *30 minutes* working time for this contest. You might be *unable* to finish all 40 questions in the time allowed.

- **Scores** Remember *this is a contest, not a test.* There is no "passing" or "failing" score. Few students score as high as 30 points (75% correct); students with even half that, 15 points, *deserve commendation!*

- **Format and Point Value** This is a multiple-choice contest. For each question, write the *capital letter* that is *in front of* the answer you choose. For each question, your answer will be one of the *capital letters* A, B, C, or D. Each question you answer correctly is worth 1 point. Unanswered questions receive no credit.

		Answers
1. $19.90 - 19.89 =$ A) 1 B) 0.1 C) 0.01 D) 0.001		1. C
2. When the price of the *Times-Herald* was increased from 25¢ to 30¢, this represented a price increase of A) 5% B) $16\frac{2}{3}\%$ C) 20% D) 25%		2. C
3. $\frac{1}{9} + \frac{2}{9} + \frac{3}{9} + \frac{4}{9} + \frac{5}{9} + \frac{6}{9} + \frac{7}{9} + \frac{8}{9} =$ A) 1 B) 4 C) 8 D) 16		3. B
4. The value of 20 nickels and 10 dimes is the same as the value of 10 nickels and _?_ dimes. A) 5 B) 15 C) 20 D) 25		4. C
5. $(10 \times 0.01) + (100 \times 0.002) + (1000 \times 0.0003) =$ A) 0.0123 B) 0.6 C) 0.06 D) 0.006		5. B
6. In the 10 by 20 rectangle illustrated at the right, the area of the shaded region is A) 200 B) 100 C) 50 D) 40	10 20	6. C
7. What is the sum of the reciprocals of 2, 3, and 6? A) 1 B) 11 C) $\frac{1}{11}$ D) 36		7. A
8. $\sqrt{1+4+1+4+1+4+1+4+1+4} =$ A) 5 B) 15 C) 25 D) 225		8. A
9. One-third of one-third equals one-half of A) $\frac{1}{2}$ B) $\frac{1}{9}$ C) $\frac{1}{18}$ D) $\frac{2}{9}$		9. D
10. Of the following, which *cannot* be expressed as the sum of two consecutive integers? A) −1 B) 0 C) 1 D) 1989		10. B
11. $35\% + 40\% =$ A) $\frac{3}{5}$ B) $\frac{3}{4}$ C) $\frac{4}{5}$ D) $\frac{5}{6}$		11. B
12. By how much does the square of the sum of the first 5 positive integers exceed the sum of the squares of the same 5 integers? A) 0 B) 15 C) 55 D) 170		12. A
13. $(2 \times 3 \times 4) \times (\frac{1}{2} + \frac{1}{3} + \frac{1}{4}) =$ A) 1 B) 3 C) 24 D) 26		13. D
14. Of the following, the least number is A) $-\frac{1}{10}$ B) $-\frac{1}{100}$ C) $-\frac{11}{100}$ D) $-\frac{11}{1000}$		14. D
15. In an isosceles right triangle, 2 angles each have a measure of A) 45° B) 60° C) 90° D) 180°		15. A

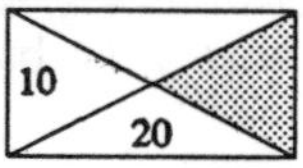

28/40 Avg 28/05

16. Roger Maris hit 61 home runs in 1961. If Maris played in 162 games that year, then, of the following, the average number of home runs Maris hit per game would be closest to A) 0.03 B) 0.38 C) 2.66 D) 32.15	16. C
17. $(2 \times 22 \times 40) - (2 \times 22 \times 39) =$ A) 22 B) 39 C) 40 D) 44	17. D
18. $\frac{98}{76 \times 54} =$ A) $\frac{0.98}{7.6 \times 5.4}$ B) $\frac{0.98}{0.76 \times 0.54}$ C) $\frac{9.8}{0.76 \times 54}$ D) $\frac{9.8}{0.76 \times 5.4}$	18. B
19. 4 hours 45 minutes before 1 P.M. is A) 5:45 A.M. B) 8:15 A.M. C) 8:45 A.M. D) 9:15 A.M.	19. B
20. 100% of 100% = A) 1 B) 2 C) 200 D) 10000	20. A
21. If p is a prime number, which of the following could also be a prime number? A) $p + 7$ B) $p + 2$ C) $p + p$ D) $p \times p$	21. B
22. When $\frac{2}{3}$ is divided by 0.33333, the quotient most nearly equals A) $\frac{2}{9}$ B) $\frac{1}{9}$ C) 1 D) 2	22. D
23. $1989 - 1989\frac{1}{2} =$ A) $\frac{1}{2}$ B) 0 C) $-\frac{1}{2}$ D) $-1\frac{1}{2}$	23. C
24. $\frac{10^8 - 1}{101} =$ A) 9999 B) 90909 C) 990099 D) 909090	24. C
25. Two CD's and three cassettes cost \$42. If 1 CD costs twice as much as 1 cassette, then the cost of 1 CD and 1 cassette is A) \$12 B) \$15 C) \$16 D) \$18	25. D
26. Which is equal to one-half of 1%? A) 0.5 B) 0.05 C) 0.005 D) 0.0005	26. B
27. If a *left angle* were defined as the supplement of a right angle, then the measure of a *left angle* would be A) 0° B) 45° C) 90° D) 180°	27. C
28. 2 m – 2 cm = A) 1.98 m B) 198 m C) 1.8 m D) 18 m	28. A
29. Mom complains she has 1 million things to do. If she takes 5 minutes to do each thing, she will be done in _?_ hours. A) 120000 B) 200000 C) $66666\frac{2}{3}$ D) $83333\frac{1}{3}$	29. D

Go on to the next page ⅢⅢ➡ **8**

30. Find the missing number: $\frac{1.21}{1.1} = \frac{1.1}{?}$ A) 1 B) 1.1 C) 10 D) 11	30. A
31. The larger square shown at the right has a perimeter of 56, and the smaller square has a perimeter of 40. What is the area of the shaded region? A) 4 B) 16 C) 20 D) 24	31. A
32. If I multiply a certain number by 100 and then add 2, the result is 1. What is this certain number? A) –1.00 B) –0.01 C) 0.01 D) 0.03	32. B
33. If $5x = x$, then $x =$ A) 0 B) 1 C) $\frac{1}{5}$ D) 5	33. A
34. Of the following, which has the greatest value? A) $\frac{\pi}{2}$ B) $\frac{\pi}{2} \times \frac{\pi}{3}$ C) $\frac{\pi}{2} \times \frac{\pi}{3} \times \frac{\pi}{4}$ D) $\frac{\pi}{3} \times \frac{\pi}{4} \times \frac{\pi}{5}$	34. D
35. The number 10 is expressible as a sum of two powers of 2; that is, $10 = 2^a + 2^b$, where a and b are whole numbers. Find $a + b$. A) 3 B) 4 C) 5 D) 6	35. B
36. A propeller 4 m long is spinning so that a point 1 m from the center is moving at 900 m/sec. How fast is the movement of a point 2 m from the center? A) 900 m/sec B) 1800 m/sec C) 2700 m/sec D) 3600 m/sec	36. B
37. A number is rounded to the nearest whole number. The original number is then rounded to the nearest ten. The difference between the 2 new numbers formed *cannot* be A) 3 B) 4 C) 5 D) 6	37.
38. The area of a square is 5. If each side of the square is tripled, the area of the new square would be A) 8 B) 15 C) 45 D) 225	38.
39. A 2 by 8 rectangle and a 3 by 7 rectangle overlap. Their common region is parallelogram P. No vertex of either rectangle is also a vertex of P. Find the least possible area of P. A) 2 B) 4 C) 6 D) 14	39.
40. The sum of the first 100 odd positive numbers is 100^2. The sum of the first 100 even positive numbers is A) 100^2 B) $100^2 + 1$ C) $100^2 + 50$ D) $100^2 + 100$	40. A

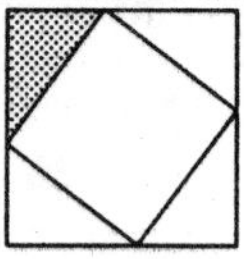

The end of the contest ✍️ **8**

Solutions on Page 133 • Answers on Page 161

1989-90 Annual 8th Grade Contest

Tuesday, February 6, 1990

8

Instructions

- **Time** You will have only *30 minutes* working time for this contest. You might be *unable* to finish all 40 questions in the time allowed.

- **Scores** Remember *this is a contest, not a test.* There is no "passing" or "failing" score. Few students score as high as 30 points (75% correct); students with even half that, 15 points, *deserve commendation!*

- **Format and Point Value** This is a multiple-choice contest. For each question, write the *capital letter* that is *in front of* the answer you choose. For each question, your answer will be one of the *capital letters* A, B, C, or D. Each question you answer correctly is worth 1 point. Unanswered questions receive no credit.

Copyright © 1990 by Mathematics Leagues Inc.

Answers

1. $\frac{1000}{1990} + \frac{900}{1990} + \frac{90}{1990} =$

   A) 0   B) 1   C) 1990   D) $\frac{1}{1990}$

   1. B

2. I arrived at Pat's house at 9:10 A.M. If I left Pat's house 360 minutes later, when did I leave Pat's house?

   A) 9:46 A.M.   B) 9:10 P.M.   C) 3:10 A.M.   D) 3:10 P.M.

   2. D

3. 0.222 + 0.333 + 0.444 =

   A) 1   B) 0.999   C) 0.99   D) 0.9

   3. B

4. Each of the following is a factor of 1990 *except*

   A) 1   B) 2   C) 5   D) 9

   4. D

5. Find the missing number: $\frac{1}{3} + \frac{1}{6} = \frac{1}{4} + ?$

   A) $\frac{1}{8}$ B) $\frac{1}{7}$ C) $\frac{1}{4}$ D) $\frac{1}{2}$

   5. C

6. (0.21 ÷ 0.07) ÷ 0.03 =

   A) 0.01   B) 1   C) 10   D) 100

   6. D

7. Find the missing number: 999 + 998 + 997 + 996 = 4000 − ?

   A) 4   B) 7   C) 10   D) 15

   7. C

8. In each of Mr. Room's five classes, the number of students is the same as the room number. His classes are held in rooms 18, 19, 20, 21, and 22. No student has two classes with Mr. Room. How many students have a class with Mr. Room?

   A) 5   B) 20   C) 100   D) 110

   8. C

9. 2 × 4 + 6 ÷ 2 =

   A) 14   B) 11   C) 10   D) 110

   9. B

10. If I add the largest whole number less than 200 to the smallest whole number greater than 200, what sum should I get?

    A) 200   B) 201   C) 300   D) 400

    10. D

11. Find the missing number: $22 \times 24 \times 26 = 11 \times 12 \times 13 \times ?$

    A) 16   B) 8   C) 6   D) 2

    11. B

12. 100% × 100% =

    A) 100%   B) 200%   C) 1000%   D) 10 000%

    12. A

13. The number 12 has six positive whole number factors. What is the product of these six factors?

    A) 12   B) 72   C) 144   D) 1728

    13. D

14. $(-5) \times (-4) \times (-3) \times (-2) \times (-1) \times (0) =$

    A) 0   B) −15   C) 120   D) −120

    14. A

15. What is the average of the two primes nearest in value to 42?

    A) 40   B) 41   C) 42   D) 43

    15. C

Go on to the next page ⏩ **8**

16. $\frac{1}{3} : \frac{1}{9} =$ A) 3:1　　B) 3:9　　C) 1:3　　D) 1:$\frac{1}{27}$	16. A
17. A pizza is cut into 8 equal slices. What is 62.5% of the pizza? A) 3 slices　B) 5 slices　C) 1/8 slice　D) 5/8 slice	17. B
18. 10.01 × 10 × 9.99 is nearest in value to A) 10　　B) 10^2　　C) 10^3　　D) 10^4	18. C
19. A string 100 m long is cut into 38 equal pieces. What is the sum of the lengths of 19 of these pieces? A) (100/38) m　B) 38 m　　C) 19 m　　D) 50 m	19. D
20. Find the missing number: 3 × 4 = 1.5 × _?_ A) 2　　B) 2.5　　C) 8　　D) 8.5	20. C
21. Which of the following numbers has the largest reciprocal? A) 0.5　　B) 1　　C) 1989　　D) 1990	21. A
22. What is the area of a circle whose circumference is 12π? A) 144π　B) 36π　　C) 9π　　D) 6π	22. B
23. A two-digit whole number is added to a three-digit whole number. What is the *least* possible value of this sum? A) 199　　B) 110　　C) 109　　D) 101	23. B
24. Of the following numbers, which is the largest? A) $\frac{80}{9}$　　B) $\sqrt{80}$　　C) $\frac{89}{10}$　　D) $\sqrt{(-9)\times(-9)}$	24. D
25. A piece of rope 4 m long weighs 3 kg. A second piece of this same rope weighs 12 kg. How long is the second piece? A) 48 m　　B) 16 m　　C) 9 m　　D) 1 m	25. B
26. In rhombus *ABCD* shown at the right, *A* is a 60° angle and *AB* = 12. What is the perimeter of triangle *ABD*? A) 12　　B) 24　　C) 36　　D) 144	26. C
27. How many prime numbers are divisible by 51? A) 0　　B) 1　　C) 3　　D) 51	27. A
28. The average of seven different positive whole numbers is 7. What is the largest possible value of any of these numbers? A) 49　　B) 43　　C) 28　　D) 20	28. C
29. Every whole number divisible by 1000 *must* also be divisible by A) 80　　B) 125　　C) 400　　D) 625	29. B

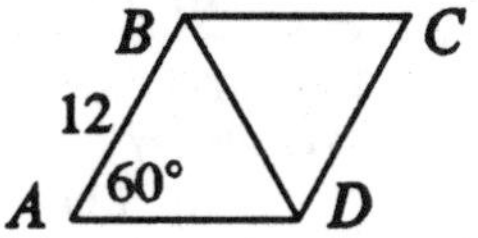

Go on to the next page ⇒   **8**

67

30. The greatest common factor of $3\times7\times13$ and $2\times5\times11$ is
A) 1 B) 2 C) 6 D) 10

30. A

31. If 12 perfectly round marbles, each 1 cm in diameter, were arranged in a straight line, touching each other, what would be the distance between the centers of the first and last marbles?
A) 10 cm B) 11 cm C) 12 cm D) 13 cm

31. B

32. $\sqrt{\dfrac{3^2+4^2}{5^2}} =$
A) 1 B) $\frac{7}{5}$ C) $\frac{12}{5}$ D) 5

32. A

33. In the rectangle at the right, the area of triangle *ABC* is 12. What is the area of triangle *ABE*?

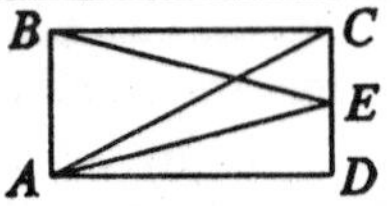

A) 18 B) 15 C) 12 D) 10

33. C

34. Find the missing number: $4^5 \times 3^5 = 6^5 \times$ _?_
A) 2 B) 6^5 C) 1^5 D) 2^5

34. D

35. In the diagram at the right, the perimeter of the larger square is 16 and the perimeter of the smaller square is 4. What is the perimeter of the entire figure?

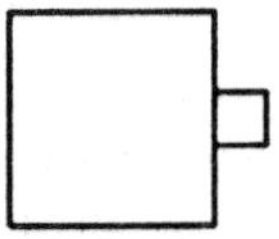

A) 18 B) 19 C) 20 D) 22

35. A

36. If twice my age minus 9 years equals half my age plus 9 years, what is my age?
A) 99 years B) 18 years C) 12 years D) 9 years

36. C

37. Two sides of a triangle have lengths 9 and 11. If no two sides of the triangle have equal lengths, the perimeter could be
A) 21 B) 23 C) 29 D) 31

37. B

38. The first 1000 primes are multiplied together. This number *must* be divisible by
A) 10 B) 100 C) 1000 D) 10^{1000}

38. A

39. If Pat is $33\frac{1}{3}\%$ taller than Lee, then Lee is what percent shorter than Pat?
A) 20% B) 25% C) 30% D) $33\frac{1}{3}\%$

39. B

40. A box-shaped refrigerator measures 12 by 10 by 7 on the outside. All six sides of the refrigerator are 1 unit thick. What is the inside volume of the refrigerator, in cubic units?
A) 840 B) 700 C) 594 D) 400

40. D

The end of the contest ✍ **8**

Solutions on Page 137 • Answers on Page 162

Aug 28/05

1990-91 Annual 8th Grade Contest

Tuesday, February 5, 1991

8

Instructions

■ **Time** You will have only *30 minutes* working time for this contest. You might be *unable* to finish all 40 questions in the time allowed.

■ **Scores** Remember *this is a contest, not a test*. There is no "passing" or "failing" score. Few students score as high as 30 points (75% correct); students with even half that, 15 points, *deserve commendation!*

■ **Format and Point Value** This is a multiple-choice contest. For each question, write the *capital letter* that is *in front of* the answer you choose. For each question, your answer will be one of the *capital letters* A, B, C, or D. Each question you answer correctly is worth 1 point. Unanswered questions receive no credit.

Copyright © 1991 by Mathematics Leagues Inc.

#	Question	Answer
1.	$1990 + 1992 =$ A) 1991 B) 2×1991 C) 1991^2 D) 1994	1. B
2.	My math class has 12 boys and 15 girls in it when everyone is present. Today, $\frac{1}{4}$ of the boys and $\frac{1}{3}$ of the girls are absent. How many students are present in my class today? A) 8 B) 19 C) 20 D) 21	2. B
3.	$0.33 + 0.033 + 0.0033 =$ A) 0.3333 B) 0.3663 C) 0.6336 D) 0.6666	3. B
4.	The square of 4 multiplied by the square root of 16 equals A) 4 B) 32 C) 64 D) 256	4. C
5.	Find the missing number: $100 = 10 \times 20 \times \underline{?}$ A) 0.1 B) 0.2 C) 0.4 D) 0.5	5. D
6.	$99 - 0.99 =$ A) 0 B) 98 C) 98.01 D) 98.1	6. C
7.	$\sqrt{4+4+4+4} =$ A) 2 B) 4 C) 8 D) 16	7. B
8.	What is the product of all the integers between −3 and 3? A) −36 B) −6 C) 0 D) 36	8. C
9.	$10^4 - 1 =$ A) 9 B) 99 C) 999 D) 9999	9. D
10.	What is the value of 99.99 rounded to the nearest tenth? A) 100.0 B) 99.99 C) 99.9 D) 99.0	10. A
11.	$(-29) - (-30) + 1 =$ A) 0 B) 1 C) 2 D) 60	11. C
12.	Of the following numbers, which is largest? A) $\frac{7}{8}$ B) $\frac{4}{5}$ C) $\frac{9}{10}$ D) $\frac{99}{100}$	12. D
13.	$\sqrt{10201} =$ A) 100 B) 101 C) 102 D) 10201	13. B
14.	$\frac{1}{2} + \frac{1}{4} + \frac{1}{8} =$ A) $\frac{3}{8}$ B) $\frac{5}{8}$ C) $\frac{7}{8}$ D) $\frac{9}{8}$	14. C
15.	The product of the two legs of a right triangle is 20. What is the triangle's area? A) 10 B) 20 C) 40 D) 200	15. A

Go on to the next page ▮▮▮➡ **8**

70

16. Find the missing exponent: $4^2 = 2^?$ A) 16 B) 8 C) 4 D) 2	16. C
17. In the diagram at the right, two parallel lines are intersected by a third line, forming a 75° angle as shown. If x and y represent the degree measures of the angles indicated, then $x + y =$ $\boxed{\begin{array}{c}75°\\x\\y\end{array}}$ A) 75° B) 90° C) 105° D) 180°	17. D
18. $\dfrac{1 \times 4 \times 9 \times 16 \times 25}{\sqrt{1} \times \sqrt{4} \times \sqrt{9} \times \sqrt{16} \times \sqrt{25}} =$ A) 24 B) 120 C) 576 D) 1440	18. B
19. $25\% \times \frac{1}{2} \times 80 =$ A) 10 B) 20 C) 40 D) 80	19. A
20. The sum of the measures of the two largest angles in a triangle *cannot* equal A) 119° B) 139° C) 159° D) 179°	20. A
21. What fraction of an hour passed between 1:55 A.M. today and 2:19 A.M. today? A) $\frac{1}{5}$ B) $\frac{2}{5}$ C) $\frac{3}{5}$ D) $\frac{4}{5}$	21. B
22. $999 \times 999 =$ A) 998001 B) 998003 C) 998007 D) 998009	22. A
23. Muffins usually cost 25¢ each. Today they are on sale for 20¢ each. If Steve has $5, how many more muffins can he buy during this sale than at the regular price? A) 2 B) 5 C) 6 D) 10	23. B
24. $(5 \times 30) \times (30 \times 5) = 15^2 \times \underline{\ ?\ }$ A) 2×5 B) $2^2 \times 5$ C) 2×5^2 D) $2^2 \times 5^2$	24. D
25. If 25% of a number equals the reciprocal of the number, the number could be A) $\frac{1}{4}$ B) $\frac{1}{2}$ C) 2 D) 4	25. C
26. $(-1)^1 + (-1)^2 + (-1)^3 + \ldots + (-1)^{1990} + (-1)^{1991} =$ A) -1 B) 0 C) 1 D) -1991	26. A
27. $1000 \times 0.1991 =$ A) 1991 B) 199.1 C) 19.91 D) 0.0001991	27. B
28. The ratio of the circumferences of two circles is 4:1. What is the ratio of the areas of these two circles? A) 2:1 B) 4:1 C) 8:1 D) 16:1	28. D
29. 12 is 150% of what number? A) 8 B) 12 C) 15 D) 18	29. A

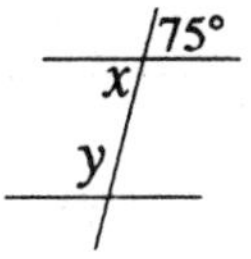

		Answers
30.	When the Health Gym had a 50% sale on membership fees, the price to join during the sale was $12 per month. What is the regular price for a 1-year membership? A) $96 B) $144 C) $288 D) $576	30. C
31.	$\frac{10+1}{20+2} = \frac{10}{20} + \underline{\ ?\ }$ A) 0 B) $\frac{1}{2}$ C) 1 D) 2	31. A
32.	Which of the following *cannot* be the lengths of the three sides of a triangle? A) 1,2,4 B) 3,4,6 C) 4,5,7 D) 5,6,8	32. A
33.	The product of an even number of odd numbers is always A) even B) odd C) prime D) negative	33. B
34.	Ali lifts 3 times the weight that Keith lifts. If Ali lifts 40 kg more than Keith, how much does Ali lift? A) 20 kg B) 40 kg C) 60 kg D) 120 kg	34. C
35.	When $2\times2\times2\times2\times2\times2\times5\times5\times5\times5\times5$ is simplified, how many zeros does the product contain? A) 2 B) 5 C) 6 D) 11	35. B
36.	The sum of the digits of a certain whole number is 7. What is the least possible value for the sum of the digits of the number which is 300 more than the original number? A) 1 B) 8 C) 10 D) 307	36. A
37.	Line segment AC is a diameter of the circle, B is on the circle, and triangle ABC is isosceles. If AC = 10, what is the area of the shaded region? A) $25\pi - 25$ B) $25\pi - 50$ C) $100\pi - 25$ D) $100\pi - 50$	37. A
38.	Which of the following numbers may be written as the sum of two consecutive whole numbers? A) 1066 B) 1492 C) 1990 D) 1991	38. D
39.	If 1 stick of lipstick costs $\frac{3}{5}$ the price of 1 bottle of nail polish, how many sticks of lipstick can be purchased for the same price as 15 bottles of nail polish? A) 5 B) 9 C) 15 D) 25	39. D
40.	If x people can do a job in d days, how long would it take y people to do the same job? A) $\frac{x}{yd}$ B) $\frac{xd}{y}$ C) $\frac{y}{xd}$ D) $\frac{yd}{x}$	40. B

The end of the contest ✍ **8**

Solutions

1982-83 Annual 7th Grade Contest
Tuesday, February 8, 1983

7

Contest Information

■ **Solutions** Turn the page for detailed contest solutions (written in the question boxes) and letter answers (in the answer columns on the right).

■ **Scores** When reviewing these questions, remember *this is a contest, not a test*. There is no "passing" or "failing" score. Few students score as high as 30 points (75% correct); students with even half that, 15 points, *deserve commendation!*

■ **Answers & Rating Scale** Turn to page 146 for the letter answers to each question and the rating scale for this contest.

		Answers
1.	$1 - \frac{1}{1983} = \frac{1983}{1983} - \frac{1}{1983} = \frac{1983-1}{1983} = \frac{1982}{1983}$. A) 0 B) $\frac{1}{1983}$ C) $\frac{1981}{1982}$ D) $\frac{1982}{1983}$	1. D
2.	$(4-3) \times (5-4) \times (6-5) \times (9-2) = 1 \times 1 \times 1 \times 7 = 7$. A) 1 B) 7 C) 10 D) 21	2. B
3.	$\sqrt{9} + \sqrt{16} = 3 + 4 = 7 = \sqrt{49}$, so choice D is correct. A) $\sqrt{5}$ B) $\sqrt{7}$ C) $\sqrt{25}$ D) $\sqrt{49}$	3. D
4.	There are 28 days; 28 days $\times$ 24 hours per day = 672 hours. A) 196 B) 696 C) 672 D) 720	4. C
5.	$125\% = 1.25 = 1\frac{1}{4} = \frac{5}{4}$. A) $\frac{4}{5}$ B) $\frac{5}{4}$ C) $\frac{6}{5}$ D) 125	5. B
6.	Since the hundredths digit is 4, round down to 43.8. A) 40 B) 44 C) 43.8 D) 43.9	6. C
7.	Since $\frac{480}{44} = \frac{120 \times 4}{11 \times 4} = \frac{120}{11}$, the correct answer is choice A. A) 120 B) 132 C) 180 D) 1920	7. A
8.	The sides forming the right angle are perpendicular. A) equal in length B) horizontal C) perpendicular D) vertical	8. C
9.	$\frac{5}{10} \times \frac{6}{10} = \frac{30}{100} = 0.30 = 0.3$ A) 30 B) 3 C) 0.3 D) 0.03	9. C
10.	If 3 times a number is 48, then the number is 16. One-fourth of 16 is 4, so choice B is correct. A) 16 B) 4 C) 12 D) 30	10. B
11.	$2^5 + 2^5 = 32 + 32 = 64 = 2^6$. A) 4^5 B) 4^{10} C) 4^{25} D) 2^6	11. D
12.	The sum of the angle measures in a triangle is 180° and in a square is 360°. The ratio is 180:360 = 1:2. A) 1:2 B) 2:3 C) 3:4 D) 4:3	12. A
13.	$0.25 + \frac{1}{2} = 0.25 + 0.50 = 0.75 = \frac{3}{4}$. A) $\frac{2}{3}$ B) $\frac{3}{4}$ C) 1 D) $1\frac{1}{4}$	13. B
14.	$0.8)\overline{17.624} = 8)\overline{176.24} = 22.03$ A) 22.3 B) 2.203 C) 2.23 D) 22.03	14. D
15.	The smallest one-digit prime is 2; the smallest two-digit prime is 11. Their product is $2 \times 11 = 22$. A) 18 B) 22 C) 26 D) 33	15. B

Go on to the next page ▸ **7**

16. Three-halves of one-half is 3/2 × 1/2 = 3/4.

   A) $\frac{3}{4}$ B) $\frac{1}{4}$ C) $\frac{2}{3}$ D) $1\frac{1}{2}$

16.
A

17. (95 × 68) − (94 × 68) = (95 − 94) × 68 = 1 × 68 = 68.

   A) 1   B) 68   C) 78   D) 88

17.
B

18. The product is ≥ 100 × 100 = 10 000 and < 1000 × 1000 = 1 000 000. The product may have either 5 or 6 digits.

   A) 3 digits   B) 5 digits   C) 7 digits   D) 9 digits

18.
B

19. The sums in the 2nd row and 4th (vertical) column are incorrect. If the number they share, 1, were changed to 3, all would be correct.

				total
9	3	2	2	16
8	2	7	1	20
2	1	4	3	10
6	8	3	5	22
total 25	14	16	13	

   A) 1   B) 2   C) 3   D) 8

19.
A

20. The fewest possible coins he could have would be 1 half-dollar, 1 quarter, 2 dimes, and 4 pennies.

   A) 0   B) 1   C) 2   D) 3

20.
A

21. $\frac{2}{0.5} + \frac{5}{0.2} = \frac{20}{5} + \frac{50}{2} = 4 + 25 = 29.$

   A) 29   B) $2\frac{1}{2}$ C) 1   D) $\frac{7}{10}$

21.
A

22. $(5\frac{1}{3}-2\frac{1}{2}) + (5\frac{1}{2}-2\frac{1}{3}) = (5\frac{1}{2}-2\frac{1}{2}) + (5\frac{1}{3}-2\frac{1}{3}) = 3 + 3 = 6.$

   A) 4   B) 5   C) 6   D) 7

22.
C

23. The dimensions of the rectangle are 3 diameters by 2 diameters or 24 by 16. The area is 24×16 = 384.

   A) 48   B) 96   C) 192   D) 384

23.
D

24. 1.4 minutes = 1.4 × 60 seconds = 84 seconds.

   A) 64 seconds   B) 84 seconds   C) 96 seconds   D) 100 seconds

24.
B

25. The least common multiple of 4, 6, and 8 is 24; all three events occur on the same day every 24 days. If all three events occur on July 1, they will next all occur together on July 25.

   A) July 9   B) July 19   C) July 24   D) July 25

25.
D

26. Using the Pythagorean Theorem in △ABD, DB = 5. Using it again in △DBC, DC = 13.

   A) 5   B) 13   C) 17   D) 18

26.
B

27. If 3 goats eat 6 tin cans in 1 hour, 6 goats eat 12 tin cans in 1 hour. So 6 goats eat 3 tin cans in 3/12 of an hour = 15 minutes.

   A) 15 minutes   B) 30 minutes   C) 1 hour   D) 2 hours

27.
A

28. Choice D is true: 45/63 < 56/63. (Use common denominators.)

   A) $\frac{1}{7} > \frac{1}{3}$ B) $\frac{2}{9} < \frac{1}{5}$ C) $\frac{2}{3} > \frac{7}{10}$ D) $\frac{5}{7} < \frac{8}{9}$

28.
D

29. $0.3\% = 0.3 \times 1/100 = 3/10 \times 1/100 = 3/1000$. A) $\frac{1}{3}$ B) $\frac{3}{10}$ C) $\frac{3}{100}$ D) $\frac{3}{1000}$	29. D
30. Since ⅔ of $9 is $6 and $9 + $6 = $15, the girl spent $9 and she had $6 left. Choice C is correct. A) $5 B) $6 C) $9 D) $10	30. C
31. Sides can *not* be 6, 6, and 12, since the sum of 2 sides of a triangle exceeds the 3rd. Sides are 6, 12, and 12; perimeter is 30. A) 18 cm B) 30 cm C) 36 cm D) 72 cm	31. B
32. $1/2 - 1/3 = 1/6$, so 20 people is one-sixth of the full room. The full room contains $6 \times 20 = 120$ people. A) 60 people B) 80 people C) 90 people D) 120 people	32. D
33. Since each number ends with 6, the product also ends with 6. A) 308 915 772 B) 308 915 774 C) 308 915 776 D) 308 915 778	33. C
34. Divide by 7: 2 *whosits* equals 5 *whatsits*. Now multiply by 10. A) 125 *whosits* B) 70 *whosits* C) 20 *whosits* D) 7 *whosits*	34. C
35. Since 88 is divisible by 8, choice B is correct. A) 15×28×33 B) 9×35×88 C) 12×77×15 D) 22×30×21	35. B
36. $\frac{1}{8} + \frac{3}{8} = \frac{4}{8} = \frac{1}{2} = \frac{3\frac{1}{2}}{7} = \frac{1}{7} + \frac{2\frac{1}{2}}{7}$, so choice C is correct. A) 3 B) 4 C) 2½ D) 3½	36. C
37. The circumferences of the gears are 48π cm and 36π cm. In 12 revolutions, the large gear turns 576π cm. Since $576\pi \div 36\pi = 16$, the smaller gear make 16 revolutions in the same time. A) 24 B) 16 C) 12 D) 9	37. B
38. Turn the diagram upside down. The shaded area is a triangle with base 2 and height 3. Its area is $\frac{1}{2} \times 2 \times 3 = 3$. A) 2 sq. units B) 3 sq. units C) 5 sq. units D) 6 sq. units	38. B
39. $\sqrt{999\,999} < \sqrt{1\,000\,000} = 1000$; desired root is slightly less. A) 3 B) 5 C) 7 D) 9	39. D
40. If the pilot flew the 1st part of the trip at full speed, it would have taken him only 2 minutes. The entire trip at full speed takes 6 minutes. 80 km in 6 minutes = 800 km in 60 minutes. A) 400 km/hr B) 600 km/hr C) 800 km/hr D) 1000 km/hr	40. C

The end of the contest 🖋 **7**

Solutions

1983-84 Annual 7th Grade Contest
Tuesday, February 14, 1984

7

Contest Information

- **Solutions** Turn the page for detailed contest solutions (written in the question boxes) and letter answers (in the answer columns on the right).

- **Scores** When reviewing these questions, remember *this is a contest, not a test*. There is no "passing" or "failing" score. Few students score as high as 30 points (75% correct); students with even half that, 15 points, *deserve commendation!*

- **Answers & Rating Scale** Turn to page 147 for the letter answers to each question and the rating scale for this contest.

1. $1 \times 9 \times 8 \times 4 = 9 \times 32 = 288.$ A) 288 B) 289 C) 984 D) 1984	1. A
2. A quadrilateral is a four-sided polygon, so choice D is correct. A) pentagon B) hexagon C) circle D) square	2. D
3. $333^2 = 333 \times 333 > 90\,000$; the ones' digit of the product is 9. A) 666 B) 999 C) 110 889 D) 333 333	3. C
4. $4\frac{1}{4} - 2\frac{1}{2} = 4\frac{1}{4} - 2\frac{2}{4} = 3\frac{5}{4} - 2\frac{2}{4} = 1\frac{3}{4}$ A) $2\frac{1}{2}$ B) $2\frac{3}{4}$ C) $1\frac{1}{4}$ D) $1\frac{3}{4}$	4. D
5. $7\,000\,000 = 7 \times 1\,000\,000$; the prime factors are 2, 5 and 7. A) 7 B) 11 C) 13 D) 17	5. A
6. $0.5 + 0.55 + 0.555 = 1.05 + 0.555 = 1.605.$ A) 0.605 B) 1.555 C) 1.605 D) 1.695	6. C
7. $(\frac{1}{2}+\frac{2}{3}+\frac{3}{4}) + (\frac{1}{2}+\frac{1}{3}+\frac{1}{4}) = (\frac{1}{2}+\frac{1}{2}) + (\frac{2}{3}+\frac{1}{3}) + (\frac{3}{4}+\frac{1}{4}) = 1 + 1 + 1.$ A) 1 B) $2\frac{1}{12}$ C) $2\frac{11}{12}$ D) 3	7. D
8. Greatest common divisor of odd numbers which differ by 2 is 1. A) 0 B) 1 C) 3 D) 5	8. B
9. $0.02 \times 0.32 = 0.0064$, so the correct answer is choice A. A) 0.0064 B) 0.064 C) 0.64 D) 64	9. A
10. The largest angle in a right triangle has a measure of 90°. A) 1° B) 89° C) 90° D) 91°	10. D
11. $\frac{1982}{1983} \div \frac{1982}{1984} = \frac{1982}{1983} \times \frac{1984}{1982} = \frac{1984}{1983} = 1\frac{1}{1983}.$ A) 1 B) $1\frac{1}{1983}$ C) $1\frac{1}{1984}$ D) 1984	11. B
12. The average of $\frac{1}{4}$ and $\frac{1}{6}$ is $(\frac{1}{4}+\frac{1}{6})\div 2 = \frac{5}{12}\div 2 = \frac{5}{12}\times\frac{1}{2} = \frac{5}{24}.$ A) $\frac{5}{12}$ B) $\frac{1}{5}$ C) $\frac{1}{10}$ D) $\frac{5}{24}$	12. D
13. $70\% = \frac{70}{100} = \frac{7}{10}$; $0.700 = \frac{700}{1000} = \frac{7}{10}$; $\frac{14}{20} = \frac{7}{10}$; but $0.07 = \frac{7}{100} \neq \frac{7}{10}.$ A) 70% B) 0.07 C) 0.700 D) $\frac{14}{20}$	13. B
14. 0 has no reciprocal; the reciprocals of $\frac{1}{2}, \frac{2}{3}$, and 1 are 2, $\frac{3}{2}$, and 1. A) 0 B) $\frac{1}{2}$ C) $\frac{2}{3}$ D) 1	14. D
15. $3^4 - 2^5 = 81 - 32 = 49 = 7^2.$ A) 6^2 B) 7^2 C) 7^1 D) 2^5	15. B

Go on to the next page ⟫ **7**

16.	$\dfrac{5 \times 10 \times 15 \times 20}{5 \times 5 \times 5 \times 5} = \dfrac{5}{5} \times \dfrac{10}{5} \times \dfrac{15}{5} \times \dfrac{20}{5} = 1 \times 2 \times 3 \times 4 = 24.$ A) 10 B) 12 C) 24 D) 750	16. C
17.	If the sum of two whole numbers is 36, their greatest possible product occurs when they both equal 18. Their product is 324. A) 35 B) 260 C) 320 D) 324	17. D
18.	If the product of two whole numbers is 36, their greatest possible sum occurs when the numbers are 1 and 36. The sum is 37. A) 12 B) 13 C) 20 D) 37	18. D
19.	$0.5 + \dfrac{5}{100} + \dfrac{1}{4} = 0.5 + 0.05 + 0.25 = 0.80 = 0.8 = \dfrac{8}{10} = \dfrac{4}{5}$ A) 0.08 B) 8 C) $\dfrac{3}{5}$ D) $\dfrac{4}{5}$	19. D
20.	Interest for a year is 12% of $800 = $96. Since 3 months is one-fourth of a year, the interest for 3 months is $\frac{1}{4} \times $96 = $24.$ A) $24 B) $32 C) $48 D) $96	20. A
21.	Divide the figure into 2 rectangles. The areas of the rectangles are 84 and 21; their sum is 105. A) 109 B) 71 C) 99 D) 105	21. D
22.	$\left(\dfrac{1}{5}\right)^2 + \dfrac{4}{5} = \dfrac{1}{25} + \dfrac{20}{25} = \dfrac{21}{25} = \dfrac{16}{25} + \dfrac{5}{25} = \left(\dfrac{4}{5}\right)^2 + \dfrac{1}{5}.$ A) $\dfrac{4}{25}$ B) $\dfrac{1}{25}$ C) $\dfrac{4}{5}$ D) $\dfrac{1}{5}$	22. D
23.	The greatest possible sum is $9+9+9+9 = 36.$ A) 1 B) 10 C) 30 D) 40	23. D
24.	If 75% of a number is 36, then 150% of it is $2 \times 36 = 72.$ A) 18 B) 48 C) 54 D) 72	24. D
25.	Perimeter is twice the sum of the lengths of 2 adjacent sides. The sum of the lengths of these adjacent sides is $\frac{1}{9} \times \frac{1}{2} = \frac{1}{18}.$ A) $\dfrac{1}{36}$ B) $\dfrac{1}{18}$ C) $\dfrac{2}{3}$ D) $\dfrac{2}{9}$	25. B
26.	Since $AB = 8$ and $AB{:}BC = 2{:}5 = 8{:}20$, $BC = 20$ and $AC = 8+20 = 28.$ A) 20 B) 24 C) 28 D) 40	26. C
27.	45 km:60 minutes $= \dfrac{45}{45}$ km$:\dfrac{60}{45}$ minutes $= 1$ km$:1\frac{1}{3}$ minutes. A) 180 seconds B) 120 seconds C) 90 seconds D) 80 seconds	27. D
28.	$1\frac{1}{4}\% = \frac{5}{4}\% = \frac{5}{4} \times \frac{1}{100} = \frac{5}{400} = \frac{1}{80}.$ A) $\dfrac{5}{4}$ B) $\dfrac{5}{40}$ C) $\dfrac{1}{80}$ D) $\dfrac{4}{500}$	28. C

Go on to the next page ▶ **7**

29. $\angle BCD = \angle BCA + \angle ACD = 60° + 90°$, so the measure of angle BCD is $150°$. A) $30°$ B) $60°$ C) $90°$ D) $150°$	29. D
30. One-half of the pupils at Churchill HS walk to school. One-fourth of one-half = one-eighth go to school by bicycle. So $1 - (\frac{1}{2} + \frac{1}{8}) = 1 - \frac{5}{8} = \frac{3}{8}$ travels by neither of these methods. A) $\frac{1}{8}$ B) $\frac{1}{4}$ C) $\frac{3}{8}$ D) $\frac{5}{8}$	30. C
31. $100\% - 99\frac{44}{100}\% = \frac{56}{100}\% = \frac{14}{25}\%$, so choice C is correct. A) $\frac{16}{25}\%$ B) $\frac{33}{50}\%$ C) $\frac{14}{25}\%$ D) $1\frac{44}{100}\%$	31. C
32. Since $15 \times 20 \times 12 = 3600$, it square root is 60. A) 6 B) 60 C) 80 D) 6000	32. B
33. The sailboat's distance from its starting point is found by the Pythagorean Theorem. $6^2 + 8^2 = 10^2$, so its distance is 10 km. A) 10 km B) 12 km C) 14 km D) 48 km	33. A
34. Pair 1 & 100, 2 & 99, . . . , 50 & 51. Each has an average of $50\frac{1}{2}$. A) 49 B) $49\frac{1}{2}$ C) 50 D) $50\frac{1}{2}$	34. D
35. Areas of squares with perimeters 12 cm and 48 cm are 9 cm^2 and 144 cm^2, respectively. Since $144 \div 9 = 16$, choice D is correct. A) 4 B) 9 C) 12 D) 16	35. D
36. $2^5 = 32$; $3^3 = 27$; $5^2 = 25$; and $2^2 \times 7 = 28$. $(32+27+25) \div 3 = 28$. A) 2^5 B) 3^3 C) 5^2 D) $2^2 \times 7$	36. D
37. The increasing numbers between 5000 and 10000 are: 5678, 5679, 5689, 5789, and 6789. There are 5 in all. A) 3 B) 4 C) 5 D) 6	37. C
38. The diameter of the circle is equal to the length of a side of the square. The area of the square is $10 \times 10 = 100$. A) 40 B) 25 C) 100 D) 400	38. C
39. In decreasing order, the numbers are: 332, 331, 323, 322, 321, 313, 312, 233, 232, 231, 223, 221, 213, 212, 133, 132, 123, and 122. A) 12 B) 16 C) 18 D) 20	39. C
40. The path consists of 4 line segments and 4 quarter-circles of radius 1 cm. The area this bounds is the area of 1 circle and the 5 squares shown. Total area = $\pi + 5$. Using $\pi = 3.14$, area = 8.14. A) 7 B) 8 C) 9 D) 10	40. B

Solutions

1984-85 Annual 7th Grade Contest

Tuesday, February 12, 1985

7

Contest Information

- **Solutions** Turn the page for detailed contest solutions (written in the question boxes) and letter answers (in the answer columns on the right).

- **Scores** When reviewing these questions, remember *this is a contest, not a test.* There is no "passing" or "failing" score. Few students score as high as 30 points (75% correct); students with even half that, 15 points, *deserve commendation!*

- **Answers & Rating Scale** Turn to page 148 for the letter answers to each question and the rating scale for this contest.

Before Computer

1.	The product of 2 odd numbers is odd, so choice B is correct. A) 1985×1984 B) 1985×1985 C) 1985×1986 D) $1985\frac{1}{1985}$	1. B
2.	Seventeen hundredths = 0.17; the correct answer is choice B. A) 1700 B) 0.17 C) 0.017 D) 0.0017	2. B
3.	$1000 = 10 \times 100$, so there are 100 tens in 1000. A) 3 B) 10 C) 100 D) 1000	3. C
4.	$(17 \times 87) + (17 \times 13) = 17 \times (87 + 13) = 17 \times 100 = 1700$. A) 1699 B) 1700 C) 1701 D) 1702	4. B
5.	Since the tenths' digit of 11.45 is 4, do *not* increase the ones' digit. (11.45 differs from 11 by 0.45 and from 12 by 0.55.) A) 11.45 B) 11.51 C) 12.18 D) 12.49	5. A
6.	$37.3 - 26.4 = (37.3 - 26.3) - 0.1 = 11 - 0.1 = 10.9$ A) 11.9 B) 9.9 C) 11.1 D) 10.9	6. D
7.	Since Mickey Mouse can file cards at the rate of 80 cards an hour, after 7 hours he has filed $7 \times 80 = 560$ cards. This leaves $800 - 560 = 240$ cards to be filed. A) 560 B) 260 C) 240 D) 140	7. C
8.	$\sqrt{1^2 + 2^2 + 2^2} = \sqrt{1 + 4 + 4} = \sqrt{9} = 3$. A) 5 B) $\sqrt{5}$ C) 3 D) 9	8. C
9.	$m\angle CBD + m\angle ABD = 180°$; since $m\angle CBD = 36°$, $m\angle ABD = 180° - 36° = 144°$. A) 144° B) 324° C) 72° D) 54°	9. A
10.	$\frac{48}{72} = \frac{24}{36} = \frac{2}{3} = 66\frac{2}{3}\%$, so choice D is correct. A) $\frac{3}{4}$ B) $\frac{5}{8}$ C) 0.65 D) $66\frac{2}{3}\%$	10. D
11.	The primes between 35 and 45 are 37, 41, and 43; there are 3. A) 1 B) 2 C) 3 D) 4	11. C
12.	$\frac{3}{2} + \frac{5}{4} + \frac{9}{8} + \frac{18}{16} = 1\frac{1}{2} + 1\frac{1}{4} + 1\frac{1}{8} + 1\frac{2}{16} = 4 + \frac{8}{16} + \frac{4}{16} + \frac{2}{16} + \frac{2}{16} = 5$. A) $4\frac{15}{16}$ B) $5\frac{1}{16}$ C) 4 D) 5	12. D
13.	$12\frac{1}{2}\% = 12.5\% = 0.125 = 1/8 \neq 12.5$ A) 12.5% B) 0.125 C) 12.5 D) $\frac{1}{8}$	13. C
14.	$0.5 \times 0.5 = 0.25 = 25/100 = 1/4$. A) $\frac{1}{25}$ B) $\frac{1}{4}$ C) $\frac{1}{5}$ D) $\frac{1}{10}$	14. B
15.	Since $C = \pi d$ (where C is the circumference and d is the diameter), the value of $C \div d$ is π. A) π B) 2π C) 2 D) 4	15. A

		Answers
16.	400% of 20 = 4.00 × 20 = 80, so choice B is correct. A) 20 B) 80 C) 500 D) 8000	16. B
17.	These numbers are the multiples of 4 between 1 and 99: 4×1, 4×2, 4×3, . . . , 4×23, and 4×24. There are 24 such numbers. A) 23 B) 24 C) 25 D) 96	17. B
18.	$\frac{0.5}{0.75} = \frac{50}{75} = \frac{2}{3} = \frac{10}{15}$, so the correct answer is choice D. A) $\frac{1}{15}$ B) $\frac{3}{15}$ C) $\frac{5}{15}$ D) $\frac{10}{15}$	18. D
19.	When 615 is divided by 7, the remainder is 6. None of the other choices has as large a remainder as this. A) 615 B) 305 C) 714 D) 1001	19. A
20.	0.003 = 0.3%, so choice B is correct. A) 3% B) 0.3% C) 0.03% D) 0.003%	20. B
21.	If the perimeter is 28 cm and area 45 sq. cm, the sum of the dimensions is 14 and the product is 45. Choice C satisfies this. A) 1 and 28 B) 3 and 15 C) 5 and 9 D) 3 and 11	21. C
22.	Only $\frac{5}{8}$ has a numerator that is more than half its denominator. A) $\frac{5}{8}$ B) $\frac{6}{12}$ C) $\frac{34}{71}$ D) $\frac{4}{9}$	22. A
23.	The cost of twelve individual eggs is 96¢ + 12¢ = 108¢. The cost of one individual egg is 108¢÷12 = 9¢. A) 10¢ B) 9¢ C) 8¢ D) 7¢	23. B
24.	$\frac{4\frac{1}{3}}{4} = \frac{4\frac{1}{3} \times 3}{4 \times 3} = \frac{13}{12}$, so the missing number is 13. A) 26 B) 13 C) 8 D) 7	24. B
25.	Since $\frac{3}{8} = \frac{1}{2} \times \frac{3}{4}$, $\frac{3}{8}$ of the number is $\frac{1}{2} \times 24 = 12$. A) 48 B) 18 C) 12 D) 6	25. C
26.	$75\% - 66\frac{2}{3}\% = \frac{3}{4} - \frac{2}{3} = \frac{9}{12} - \frac{8}{12} = \frac{1}{12}$. A) $\frac{1}{12}$ B) $\frac{1}{8}$ C) $\frac{1}{6}$ D) $\frac{1}{4}$	26. A
27.	$\frac{5}{0.01} = \frac{500}{1} = 500$, so choice B is correct. A) 0.49 B) $\frac{5}{0.01}$ C) $3 \times \frac{1}{8}$ D) $\frac{3+6}{18}$	27. B
28.	The perimeter of the square (as well as the pentagon) is 4×15 = 60. A pentagon has 5 sides; for this regular pentagon, the length of each side is 60÷5 = 12. A) 3 cm B) $7\frac{1}{2}$ cm C) 10 cm D) 12 cm	28. D
29.	$2^4 \times 4^2 = 16 \times 16 = 256 = 4^4$. A) 6 × 6 B) 8^6 C) 8^8 D) 4^4	29. D

30. All 100 integers from 400 to 499 begin with 4. In addition, 304, 314, 324, 334, 344, 354, 364, 374, 384, and 394 end with 4. A) 100 B) 110 C) 120 D) 140	30. B
31. The 1985th even positive integer is $2 \times 1985 = 3970$. A) 1986 B) 3968 C) 3970 D) 3972	31. C
32. If the square has sides of length 10, its area is 100. When decreased 50%, length is 5 and area is 25, a decrease of 75%. A) 100% B) 75% C) 50% D) 25%	32. B
33. $1.01 = \frac{101}{100}$; its reciprocal is $\frac{100}{101}$. A) 0.101 B) 1.01 C) 0.99 D) $\frac{100}{101}$	33. D
34. Since 20% − 10% = 10%, 10% of the number is 1. If 10% of the number is 1, then 40% of the number equals $4 \times 1 = 4$. A) 4 B) 8 C) 40 D) 80	34. A
35. $\dfrac{\frac{1}{2} + \frac{1}{3}}{1 - \frac{1}{2} \times \frac{1}{3}} = (\frac{3}{6} + \frac{2}{6}) \div (1 - \frac{1}{6}) = \frac{5}{6} \div \frac{5}{6} = 1.$ A) 0 B) 1 C) $\frac{6}{25}$ D) 5	35. B
36. $m\angle ABD = m\angle DBY - m\angle ABY =$ $180° - 45° = 135°$ A) 270° B) 45° C) 135° D) 90°	36. C
37. $1985 - 1984 = 1$; $\frac{1}{1984} - \frac{1}{1985}$ is less than $\frac{1}{1000000}$. A) 1 B) $\frac{1985}{1984}$ C) $\frac{1984}{1985}$ D) $\frac{1}{1984}$	37. A
38. Since 5 cars plus 8 trucks take up the same room as 11 trucks, 5 cars take up the same room as 3 trucks. Multiply by 10: 50 cars take up the same room as 30 trucks. A) 18 B) 30 C) 50 D) 80	38. C
39. $(3*4)*5 = (\frac{7}{12})*5 = \dfrac{\frac{7}{12} + 5}{\frac{7}{12} \times 5} = (\frac{7}{12} + \frac{60}{12}) \div \frac{35}{12} = \frac{67}{12} \times \frac{12}{35} = \frac{67}{35}.$ A) $\frac{35}{12}$ B) $\frac{67}{420}$ C) $\frac{1}{35}$ D) $\frac{67}{35}$	39. D
40. In choice D, the two squares "topmost" in the drawing would have to overlap; only 5 of a cube's 6 faces would be covered. A) B) C) D)	40. D

The end of the contest ✍   **7**

Solutions

1985-86 Annual 7th Grade Contest
Tuesday, February 11, 1986

7

Contest Information

■ **Solutions** Turn the page for detailed contest solutions (written in the question boxes) and letter answers (in the answer columns on the right).

■ **Scores** When reviewing these questions, remember *this is a contest, not a test*. There is no "passing" or "failing" score. Few students score as high as 30 points (75% correct); students with even half that, 15 points, *deserve commendation!*

■ **Answers & Rating Scale** Turn to page 149 for the letter answers to each question and the rating scale for this contest.

		Answers
1.	A fraction with a denominator of 1 is equal to its numerator. A) $\frac{1986}{1}$ B) $\frac{1986}{1986}$ C) 1987 D) $\frac{1}{1986}$	1. A
2.	$6666 + 4444 = 11\,110$, so choice D is correct. A) 10 000 B) 10 110 C) 11 010 D) 11 110	2. D
3.	Carol bought 10 pens at 89¢ per pen, so they cost \$8.90. Since \$10 − \$8.90 = \$1.10, choice A is correct. A) \$1.10 B) 79¢ C) \$9.11 D) \$2.10	3. A
4.	$8080 − 7979 = (8000 − 7900) + (80 − 79) = 100 + 1 = 101.$ A) 111 B) 101 C) 1001 D) 1111	4. B
5.	$0.3 = 30\%$; this is nearest in value to 25%. A) 50% B) 40% C) 25% D) 20%	5. C
6.	$4 + 3 × (8 − 4) = 4 + 3 × 4 = 4 + 12 = 16.$ A) 52 B) 28 C) 24 D) 16	6. D
7.	Each angle is 90°; the sum of the measures of any 3 is 270°. A) 90° B) 180° C) 270° D) 360°	7. C
8.	$2\frac{2}{3} + \frac{2}{3} = 2\frac{4}{3} = 3\frac{1}{3}$ A) 2 B) $3\frac{1}{3}$ C) $3\frac{1}{2}$ D) $3\frac{2}{3}$	8. B
9.	$511÷7 = 73$; since 73 is prime, it's the missing factor. A) 53 B) 63 C) 73 D) 83	9. C
10.	$0.2 × 0.2 = 0.04$, so choice D is correct. A) 4 B) $\frac{1}{4}$ C) 0.4 D) 0.04	10. D
11.	Every 7 days is a Tuesday; $777 = 7×111$, so it's a Tuesday. A) Monday B) Tuesday C) Wednesday D) Thursday	11. B
12.	$\frac{3}{14} × \frac{7}{15} = \frac{3 × 7}{14 × 15} = \frac{3}{15} × \frac{7}{14} = \frac{1}{5} × \frac{1}{2} = \frac{1}{10}.$ A) $\frac{2}{5}$ B) $\frac{1}{10}$ C) $\frac{5}{2}$ D) 10	12. B
13.	A right triangle has 1 angle of measure 90° and 2 angles of measure less than 90°. Only choice A is ≤ 90°. A) 89° B) 91° C) 93° D) 95°	13. A
14.	$20 × 30 × 40 = (2 × 3 × 4) × (10 × 10 × 10) = 24 × 1000.$ A) 12 × 200 B) 24 × 1000 C) 6 × 400 D) 40 × 6000	14. B
15.	One-tenth of one-tenth $= \frac{1}{10} × \frac{1}{10} = \frac{1}{100}$, so choice A is correct. A) $\frac{1}{100}$ B) $\frac{1}{20}$ C) $\frac{1}{5}$ D) 1	15. A
16.	$49.5÷0.5 = 495÷5 = 99$; choice D is most nearly equal to this. A) 10 B) 25 C) 50 D) 100	16. D

Go on to the next page ⫸ 7

Answers

17. $\frac{99}{999} = \frac{9 \times 11}{9 \times 111} = \frac{9}{9} \times \frac{11}{111} = 1 \times \frac{11}{111} = \frac{11}{111}.$

   A) $\frac{1}{11}$ B) $\frac{1}{10}$ C) $\frac{1}{9}$ D) $\frac{11}{111}$

17.
D

18. $\sqrt{9} \times \sqrt{9} = 3 \times 3 = 9 = 9 \times 1$, so the missing number is 1.

   A) 1   B) 3   C) 6   D) 9

18.
A

19. Choice A differs from 1 by 0.01; no other choice is as close.

   A) $\frac{99}{100}$ B) $1\frac{1}{99}$ C) 0.9   D) 1.1

19.
A

20. If area is 24 m^2 and perimeter is 20 m, the product of the dimensions is 24 and the sum is 10; lengths are 4 and 6.

   A) 10 m   B) 8 m   C) 6 m   D) 5 m

20.
C

21. $\frac{1}{4} + \frac{1}{3} = \frac{3}{12} + \frac{4}{12} = \frac{7}{12}$;

   this leaves $1 - \frac{7}{12} =$

   $\frac{5}{12}$ for region C.

   A) $\frac{1}{2}$ B) $\frac{5}{7}$ C) $\frac{11}{12}$ D) $\frac{5}{12}$

21.
D

22. $\frac{0.1}{5} = \frac{0.1 \times 10}{5 \times 10} = \frac{1}{50}$

   A) $\frac{1}{50}$ B) $\frac{1}{5}$ C) $\frac{1}{2}$ D) 5

22.
A

23. If half of the 24 people leave, 12 leave. If half of those who left return, 6 return. There are now $24 - 12 + 6 = 18$ people.

   A) 6   B) 12   C) 18   D) 24

23.
C

24. $5 \times 6 \times 7 \times 8 \times \frac{1}{5} \times \frac{1}{6} \times \frac{1}{7} \times \frac{1}{8} = (5 \times \frac{1}{5}) \times (6 \times \frac{1}{6}) \times (7 \times \frac{1}{7}) \times (8 \times \frac{1}{8}) = 1$.

   A) 0   B) 1   C) 4   D) 8

24.
B

25. To nearest tenth, 0.999 is between 0.9 and 1.0; it is closer to 1.0.

   A) 0.1   B) 0.9   C) 0.99   D) 1.0

25.
D

26. $\frac{3}{8} - \frac{1}{8} = \frac{2}{8} = \frac{1}{4}$; so when 8 liters are added, $\frac{1}{4}$ of the tank = 8 liters. The capacity of the tank is $\frac{4}{4} = 4 \times 8 = 32$ liters.

   A) 16 liters   B) 24 liters   C) 32 liters   D) 40 liters

26.
C

27. If 20% of a number is 20, 100% of the number is $5 \times 20 = 100$.

   A) 4   B) 5   C) 40   D) 100

27.
D

28. Since 30:15 = 150:75, the shadow would be 75 m.

   A) 3 m   B) 30 m   C) 75 m   D) 135 m

28.
C

29. Since $33\frac{1}{3}\%$ of $66\frac{2}{3}\% = \frac{1}{3} \times \frac{2}{3} = \frac{2}{9} = 0.222...$, choice A is closest.

   A) 22%   B) 33%   C) 50%   D) 100%

29.
A

Go on to the next page ⫸ 7

30. There are 15 boys in the classroom. If there were 5 girls in the room, there would be 3 times as many boys in the room as girls. Since 21 − 16 = 5, 16 girls must leave the room. A) 5　　　B) 6　　　C) 16　　　D) 18	30. C
31. Split the diagram into 2 rectangles, as shown at the right. Then, half of each rectangle is occupied by the triangle. So area of $\triangle AED$ = ½×24 = 12. 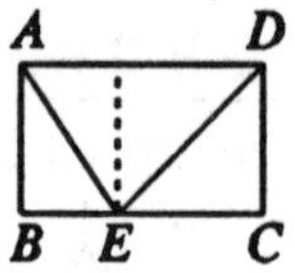 A) 16　　　B) 15　　　C) 12　　　D) 6	31. C
32. If the period of 45 consecutive days begins with a Monday, there will be a total of 7 Mondays that occur in 45 days. A) 5　　　B) 6　　　C) 7　　　D) 9	32. C
33. Adding (■ × ■) to ▼ yields ▼, so ■ × ■ = 0. Thus, ■ = 0. A) −1　　　B) 0　　　C) $\frac{1}{2}$　　　D) 1	33. B
34. If the average of three numbers is 67, their sum is 3×67 = 201. Since 56 + 91 = 147, the third number is 201 − 147 = 54. A) 34　　　B) 44　　　C) 52　　　D) 54	34. D
35. If the difference between two prime numbers is odd, one of them must be even. The primes are 2 and 2 + 1985 = 1987. A) 2431　　　B) 2002　　　C) 1987　　　D) 1986	35. C
36. One-third of 45 is 15 and 15 + 45 = 60, so choice B is correct. A) 40　　　B) 45　　　C) 80　　　D) 180	36. B
37. One slice's perimeter = (lengths of 2 radii) + (⅛ of the circumference of whole pizza). Perimeter = 2×8 + ⅛×16π = 16 + 2π. A) 16 + 2π　　B) 2π　　　C) 8π　　　D) 8 + 4π	37. A
38. If the square has sides of length 10, its area is 100. When increased by 50%, length is 15 and area is 225; increase is 125%. A) 50%　　　B) 100%　　　C) 125%　　　D) 225%	38. C
39. $2^7 \times 5^6 = 2 \times 2^6 \times 5^6 = 2 \times (2 \times 5)^6 = 2 \times 10^6 = 2\,000\,000$. A) 2 000 000　B) 1 280 000　C) 2 555 555　D) 5 200 200	39. A
40. 2! = 2, 3! = 6, 4! = 24, and 5! = 120. Since 120 is a factor from then on, the units' digits of all the rest are 0. The units' digit of the sum is the units' digit of 2+6+24+120; this is a 2. A) 0　　　B) 1　　　C) 2　　　D) 3	40. C

The end of the contest ✍ **7**

Solutions

1986-87 Annual 7th Grade Contest

Tuesday, February 10, 1987

7

Contest Information

- **Solutions** Turn the page for detailed contest solutions (written in the question boxes) and letter answers (in the answer columns on the right).

- **Scores** When reviewing these questions, remember *this is a contest, not a test.* There is no "passing" or "failing" score. Few students score as high as 30 points (75% correct); students with even half that, 15 points, *deserve commendation!*

- **Answers & Rating Scale** Turn to page 150 for the letter answers to each question and the rating scale for this contest.

1. $1 + 9 + 87 = 97$, which is an odd number. A) $1+9+87$ B) $1 \times 98 \times 7$ C) 198^7 D) $19+87$	1. A
2. $3^2 + 4^2 - 5^2 = 9 + 16 - 25 = 0$, so choice A is correct. A) 0 B) 2 C) 4 D) 8	2. A
3. $3 \times 4 \times 5 = 60 = 20 + 40 = (4 \times 5) + (8 \times 5)$; choice D is correct. A) 3 B) 3×5 C) 8 D) 8×5	3. D
4. $\frac{6}{7} \times \frac{7}{8} \times \frac{8}{9} = 6 \times \frac{7}{7} \times \frac{8}{8} \times \frac{1}{9} = 6 \times \frac{1}{9} = \frac{6}{9} = \frac{2}{3}$. A) $\frac{1}{3}$ B) $\frac{2}{3}$ C) $\frac{6}{504}$ D) 1	4. B
5. If the sum of two numbers is 100 and one of the numbers is 2 more than the other, the numbers are 49 and 51. A) 50 B) 51 C) 52 D) 53	5. B
6. $0.06 = \frac{6}{100} = \frac{3}{50} \neq \frac{3}{5}$, so choice D is correct. A) $\frac{6}{10}$ B) $\frac{33}{55}$ C) 60% D) 0.06	6. D
7. The largest angle in the isosceles triangle is a 100° angle, so the sum of the measures of the other 2 angles is 80°; each is 40°. A) 40° B) 50° C) 80° D) 180°	7. A
8. $225\% = \frac{225}{100} = \frac{9}{4} = 2\frac{1}{4}$. A) $\frac{225}{1000}$ B) $\frac{1}{4}$ C) 22.5 D) $2\frac{1}{4}$	8. D
9. If the bell rings every 2 seconds and the bird chirps every 3 seconds, the ring and chirp occur together every 6 seconds. So they occur together again in multiples of 6 seconds; $42 = 7 \times 6$. A) 40 seconds B) 41 seconds C) 42 seconds D) 43 seconds	9. C
10. $\frac{1}{4} + \frac{3}{4} = \frac{4}{4} = \frac{2}{2} = \frac{1}{2} + \frac{1}{2}$; the missing number is 1. A) 1 B) 2 C) 3 D) 4	10. A
11. $\frac{0.55}{2} = 0.55 \div 2 = 0.275$; the correct answer is choice D. A) 1.10 B) 27.5 C) 2.75 D) 0.275	11. D
12. Both 1986 and 1988 are divisible by 2; 1985 is divisible by 5. A) 1985 B) 1986 C) 1987 D) 1988	12. C
13. $(5 \times \frac{1}{1000}) + (4 \times \frac{1}{100}) + (3 \times \frac{1}{10}) = 0.005 + 0.04 + 0.3 = 0.345$. A) 0.345 B) 0.435 C) 0.534 D) 0.543	13. A
14. Since the area of the rectangle is 36, the length of a side of the square is 6 and its perimeter is 24. A) 6 B) 24 C) 26 D) 36	14. B
15. If 10 zigs = 6 zags, then $\frac{10}{10}$ zigs = $\frac{6}{10}$ zags or 1 zig = $\frac{3}{5}$ zags. A) $\frac{3}{5}$ zags B) $\frac{2}{3}$ zags C) $1\frac{3}{5}$ zags D) $1\frac{2}{3}$ zags	15. A

16. 1 hour = 60×60 = 3600 seconds; 1 second:1 hour = 1:3600. A) $\frac{1}{7200}$ B) $\frac{1}{3600}$ C) $\frac{1}{1440}$ D) $\frac{1}{60}$	16. B
17. 0.48÷0.016 = 480÷16 = 30, so choice C is correct. A) 0.3 B) 3 C) 30 D) 300	17. C
18. If the average of 3 numbers is between 7 and 10, the sum of the numbers is between 3×7 = 21 and 3×10 = 30. A) 20 B) 22 C) 26 D) 28	18. A
19. Numerator of choice C is less than one-half its denominator. A) $\frac{99}{197}$ B) $\frac{1}{2}$ C) $\frac{49}{99}$ D) $\frac{100}{199}$	19. C
20. If 2 cm represents 50 meters, then (2÷10) cm represents (50÷10) meters; so 0.2 cm represents 5 meters. A) 10 B) 0.02 C) 0.2 D) $\frac{1}{10}$	20. C
21. If the measures of the angles of a triangle are consecutive integers, the measures are 59°, 60°, and 61°. A) 1° B) 59° C) 60° D) 180°	21. B
22. $\frac{1}{3} \div \frac{3}{4} = \frac{1}{3} \times \frac{4}{3} = \frac{4}{9}$, so $\frac{1}{3} = \frac{3}{4} \times \frac{4}{9}$. A) $\frac{1}{4}$ B) $\frac{9}{4}$ C) $\frac{5}{12}$ D) $\frac{4}{9}$	22. D
23. Values of choices A, B, C, & D are 12, 0, 3, & 15 respectively. A) $2 \times [9 - (6 - 3)]$ B) $2 \times [(9 - 6) - 3]$ C) $[2 \times (9 - 6)] - 3$ D) $(2 \times 9) - (6 - 3)$	23. D
24. $18 \div 4\frac{1}{2} = 18 \div \frac{9}{2} = 18 \times \frac{2}{9} = \frac{36}{9} = 4$. A) $\frac{1}{81}$ B) $\frac{1}{4}$ C) 4 D) 81	24. C
25. The third side is 8 since the sum of any two sides of a triangle is greater than the third side. Perimeter = 2 + 8 + 8 = 18. A) 10 B) 12 C) 18 D) 22	25. C
26. $5\frac{3}{4} \div \frac{1}{8} = \frac{23}{4} \times 8 = 23 \times \frac{8}{4} = 23 \times 2 = 46$. A) 46 B) 43 C) 40 D) 6	26. A
27. It takes 1500÷10 = 150 cartons with 10 books per carton; it takes 1500÷15 = 100 cartons with 15 books per carton. A) 5 B) 50 C) 100 D) 500	27. B
28. If $a \blacktriangle b = a + a + b + b$, then $2 \blacktriangle 3 = 2 + 2 + 3 + 3 = 10$. A) 6 B) 10 C) 12 D) 13	28. B
29. $\left(\left(\left(\frac{1}{2} \div \frac{1}{3}\right) \div \frac{1}{4}\right) \div \frac{1}{4}\right) = \left(\frac{12}{2} \div \frac{1}{4}\right) = 6 \times 4 = 24$. A) $\frac{1}{48}$ B) 24 C) 48 D) 96	29. B

Go on to the next page ⏭ **7**

30. Since $\frac{1}{3} > (\frac{1}{3})^2 = \frac{1}{9}$, choice B is correct. A) 0, 0 B) $\frac{1}{3}, \frac{1}{3}$ C) $\frac{1}{2}, \frac{1}{4}$ D) $\frac{1}{2}, 0$	30. B
31. $\frac{10}{14} = \frac{5}{7} = \sqrt{\frac{25}{49}}$, so the correct answer is choice C. A) 7 B) 35 C) 49 D) 196	31. C
32. If each person served on *one* 3-person committee, there would be $24 \div 3 = 8$ committees. There are $4 \times 8 = 32$ committees. A) 32 B) 24 C) 18 D) 12	32. A
33. As shown in the diagram, $AB = BC = CD$, so AC is 200% of CD. 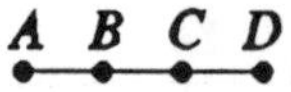 **A B C D** A) 25% B) 50% C) 100% D) 200%	33. D
34. Of every 5 people in the class, 2 are under 12 and 3 are 12 or over. Since 3 of every 5 students are 12 years old or over, the percent is 60% and the correct answer is choice C. A) $33\frac{1}{3}\%$ B) 40% C) 60% D) $66\frac{2}{3}\%$	34. C
35. The product $12 \times$ integer $= 2^2 \times 3 \times$ integer. This product is a perfect square only if one of the integer's factors is a 3. A) 2 B) 3 C) 4 D) 12	35. B
36. The volume of cube I is $10^3 = 1000$. The volume of cube II is $1000 + 331 = 1331$. Since $11^3 = 1331$, cube II's edge is 11. A) 14 meters B) 13 meters C) 12 meters D) 11 meters	36. D
37. Since $\sqrt{64}$ is the smallest choice, its reciprocal is largest. A) $\sqrt{64}$ B) 64 C) 64^2 D) 64^3	37. A
38. Each revolution the wheel moves $\pi \times 2$ meters. Using $\pi = 3.14$, it moves 6.28 m/revolution; $100 \div 6.28$ is closest to choice C. A) 64 B) 32 C) 16 D) 8	38. C
39. I earned $6, Ron earned $3, and Mary earned $2 of each $11 earned. The most I earned was the largest amount less than $(\frac{6}{11}) \times \$125$; so choice C is correct. A) $54 B) $60 C) $66 D) $72	39. C
40. Action Comic #1 has increased in value 1 849 990¢. The percent increase is $\frac{1849990}{10} \times 100\% = 18\ 499\ 900\%$. A) 18 500 000% B) 185 000% C) 1 849 990% D) 18 499 900%	40. D

The end of the contest ✍🏻 **7**

Solutions

1987-88 Annual 7th Grade Contest

Tuesday, February 2, 1988

7

Contest Information

- **Solutions** Turn the page for detailed contest solutions (written in the question boxes) and letter answers (in the answer columns on the right).

- **Scores** When reviewing these questions, remember *this is a contest, not a test*. There is no "passing" or "failing" score. Few students score as high as 30 points (75% correct); students with even half that, 15 points, *deserve commendation!*

- **Answers & Rating Scale** Turn to page 151 for the letter answers to each question and the rating scale for this contest.

1.	100 quarters = (100÷4) dollars = 25 dollars. A) 4 B) 25 C) 40 D) 2500	1. B
2.	$1988 - \frac{1987}{1988} = 1987\frac{1988}{1988} - \frac{1987}{1988} = 1987\frac{1988 - 1987}{1988} = 1987\frac{1}{1988}$. A) $1988\frac{1}{1988}$ B) $1988\frac{1987}{1988}$ C) $1987\frac{1}{1988}$ D) $1987\frac{1987}{1988}$	2. C
3.	0% of $\frac{44}{7} = 0 \times \frac{44}{7} = 0 = \frac{0}{7}$. A) $\frac{44}{7}$ B) $\frac{22}{7}$ C) $\frac{11}{7}$ D) $\frac{0}{7}$	3. D
4.	The total time Pat spent doing homework was 20 minutes + 25 minutes + 20 minutes + 15 minutes = 80 minutes = 1 hour and 20 minutes = $1\frac{1}{3}$ hours. A) $1\frac{1}{5}$ hours B) $1\frac{1}{4}$ hours C) $1\frac{1}{3}$ hours D) $1\frac{1}{2}$ hours	4. C
5.	$\frac{1}{4} \div \frac{1}{8} = \frac{1}{4} \times \frac{8}{1} = \frac{8}{4} = 2$. A) 32 B) 2 C) $\frac{1}{2}$ D) $\frac{1}{32}$	5. B
6.	$\sqrt{25 \times 25} = \sqrt{25^2} = 25$. A) 625 B) 25 C) 10 D) 5	6. B
7.	Since $AC = BC$, $\angle A = \angle B$. $\angle A + \angle B$ = 180° - $\angle C$ = 180° - 60° = 120°. So $\angle B$ = 120°÷2 = 60°. A) 60° B) 45° C) 30° D) 12°	7. A
8.	50% of $\frac{1}{6} = \frac{1}{2} \times \frac{1}{6} = \frac{1}{12}$. A) $\frac{1}{2}$ B) $\frac{1}{3}$ C) $\frac{1}{9}$ D) $\frac{1}{12}$	8. D
9.	If I walk around this lot once, I walk a distance equal to the perimeter of the lot; perimeter = 2×(42 m + 26 m) = 136 m. A) 68 m B) 104 m C) 136 m D) 272 m	9. C
10.	22% of 99 = 0.22 × 99 = 22 × 0.99 = 0.99 × 22 = 99% of 22. A) 0.22 B) 2.2 C) 22 D) 220	10. C
11.	50.050 − 0.005 = 50.040 + (0.010 − 0.005) = 50.040 + 0.005 = 50.045. A) 50.045 B) 50.055 C) 49.945 D) 49.045	11. A
12.	$\frac{88}{88} - \frac{19}{19} = 1 - 1 = 0$. A) 0 B) 1 C) $\frac{69}{88}$ D) $\frac{69}{19}$	12. A
13.	A side of the larger square is 5 and a side of the smaller square is 4. Their areas are 25 and 16; the area of the region between the two squares is 25 − 16 = 9. A) 1 B) 2 C) 4 D) 9	13. D
14.	$\frac{1}{6} + \frac{2}{6} = \frac{3}{6} = \frac{1}{2}$; since $\frac{2}{6} = \frac{1}{3}$, choice B is correct. A) $\frac{1}{4}$ B) $\frac{1}{3}$ C) $\frac{1}{2}$ D) $\frac{1}{6}$	14. B

15. $8.34 + 7.13 = 15.47$; when rounded to the nearest tenth, this becomes 15.5. A) 15.47 B) 15.4 C) 15.5 D) 20	15. C
16. $10\% \div 100 = 0.1 \div 100 = 0.001$, so choice A is correct. A) $\frac{1}{1000}$ B) $\frac{1}{100}$ C) $\frac{1}{10}$ D) 10	16. A
17. 44 fortnights $\times 2 = 88$ weeks; 88 weeks $\times 7 = 616$ days. A) 88 days B) 154 days C) 308 days D) 616 days	17. D
18. $3 \times (\frac{5}{3} + \frac{7}{3} + \frac{9}{3}) = 3 \times \frac{21}{3} = 21$. A) 7 B) 21 C) 63 D) $\frac{7}{3}$	18. B
19. If 2 cm represents 50 km, 1 cm represents 25 km. So their actual distance apart is $7.5 \times 25 = 187.5$ km. A) 375 km B) 275 km C) 187.5 km D) 75 km	19. C
20. $\frac{1}{2} \times \frac{1}{4} \times 9876 = \frac{1 \times 1}{2 \times 4} \times 9876 = \frac{1}{8} \times 9876$. A) 9876 B) 4938 C) 2469 D) 1234	20. A
21. $\angle 1 + \angle 2 + \angle ABC = 180°$. Since $\triangle ABC$ is an equilateral triangle, $\angle ABC = 60°$. So $\angle 1 + \angle 2 + 60° = 180°$, $\angle 1 + \angle 2 = 120°$. A) 60° B) 90° C) 120° D) 180°	21. C
22. The sum of a positive number and its reciprocal is $\geq 2 > 1.9$. A) 0 B) 1 C) 2 D) more than 1.9	22. D
23. The ticket price was $180 - 18 = 162$. Since the cashier reduced the ticket price by 20%, Jan's cost for the TV was $162 - (0.2 \times 162) = 162 - 32.40 = 129.60$. A) $162 B) $129.60 C) $126 D) $120	23. B
24. The number of eighths in $7.75 = 7.75 \div \frac{1}{8} = 7.75 \times 8 = 62$. A) 10 B) 31 C) 59 D) 62	24. D
25. Undo each operation: $\frac{3}{8} \times 6 = \frac{18}{8}$; $\frac{18}{8} \div 5 = \frac{18}{40} = \frac{9}{20}$. A) $\frac{5}{16}$ B) $\frac{5}{6}$ C) $\frac{6}{5}$ D) $\frac{9}{20}$	25. D
26. Since $248¢ \div 5¢$ has a quotient of 49, the answer is choice B. A) 9 B) 49 C) 50 D) 245	26. B
27. $\frac{1}{2} : 8 = (2 \times \frac{1}{2}) : (2 \times 8) = 1:16$, so choice A is correct. A) 1:16 B) 1:6 C) $2:\frac{1}{8}$ D) $\frac{1}{2}:4$	27. A
28. Area of shaded region = area of rectangle − area of triangle = $40 - 6 = 34$. A) 6 B) 12 C) 28 D) 34	28. D

29. $(0.3)^2 = 0.09$; $\sqrt{0.09} = 0.3$; $0.5 \times 0.5 = 0.25$; choice B is largest. A) $(0.3)^2$ B) $\sqrt{0.09}$ C) 0.5×0.5 D) 0.09	29. B
30. 30 cm $= 0.3$ m and 20 cm $= 0.2$ m; area $= 0.3 \times 0.2 = 0.06$ m^2. A) 0.06 m^2 B) 0.6 m^2 C) 6 m^2 D) 600 m^2	30. A
31. Add 3 to both numerator and denominator: $\frac{1+3}{3+3} = \frac{4}{6} = \frac{2}{3}$. A) 1 B) 2 C) 3 D) 4	31. C
32. If the average of 3 numbers is between 5 and 8, then their sum is between $3 \times 5 = 15$ and $3 \times 8 = 24$; choice D is unattainable. A) $15\frac{1}{3}$ B) 16 C) $20\frac{3}{4}$ D) 25	32. D
33. $[(0.3)^2 + (0.4)^2]^2 = [0.09 + 0.16]^2 = [0.25]^2 = 0.0625$. A) 25 B) 6.25 C) 0.625 D) 0.0625	33. D
34. $\sqrt{\sqrt{16}} = \sqrt{4} = 2$, so choice B is correct. A) 1 B) 2 C) 4 D) 8	34. B
35. $28 \times 5\frac{1}{2} = (28 \times 5) + (28 \times \frac{1}{2}) = (20 \times 5) + (8 \times 5) + (28 \times \frac{1}{2})$. A) $(28 \times 50) + (28 \times \frac{1}{2})$ B) $(20 \times 5) + (8 \times 5) + (28 \times \frac{1}{2})$ C) $(20 \times 50) + (8 \times 5\frac{1}{2})$ D) $(28 \times \frac{1}{2}) + (8 \times 5\frac{1}{2}) + (20 \times 5)$	35. B
36. Each side of the triangle can intersect the parallelogram at most 2 times. Since $3 \times 2 = 6$, the correct answer is choice D. A) 3 points B) 4 points C) 5 points D) 6 points	36. D
37. $900^2 < 999^2 < 1000^2$ or $810\,000 < 999^2 < 1\,000\,000$; so $10^5 < 999^2 < 10^6$. A) 10^3 and 10^4 B) 10^4 and 10^5 C) 10^5 and 10^6 D) 10^6 and 10^7	37. C
38. The sum of the first 1 million primes consists of 1 even number, 2, and 999 999 odd numbers. This sum is odd. A) 1 B) 2 C) 3 D) 9	38. B
39. The product of 65 and 120 is divisible by 100; the tens' digit is 0. A) 0 B) 5 C) 7 D) 9	39. A
40. The sum of the first 100 positive whole numbers is 5050, and the 101st positive whole number is 101. Therefore, the 101st triangular number is the sum of the 100th triangular number and 101. So the 101st triangular number is $5050 + 101 = 5151$. A) 5051 B) 5150 C) 5151 D) 5250	40. C

The end of the contest 🖘 **7**

Solutions

1988-89 Annual 7th Grade Contest

Tuesday, February 7, 1989

7

Contest Information

- **Solutions** Turn the page for detailed contest solutions (written in the question boxes) and letter answers (in the answer columns on the right).

- **Scores** When reviewing these questions, remember *this is a contest, not a test*. There is no "passing" or "failing" score. Few students score as high as 30 points (75% correct); students with even half that, 15 points, *deserve commendation!*

- **Answers & Rating Scale** Turn to page 152 for the letter answers to each question and the rating scale for this contest.

1. 9876 + 543 + 21 = 10440, so choice D is correct. A) 10100　　B) 12340　　C) 10340　　D) 10440	1. D
2. $\frac{1989}{1987} = 1\frac{2}{1987}$, so choice A is the largest of the four choices. A) $\frac{1989}{1987}$　　B) $\frac{1989}{1988}$　　C) $\frac{1989}{1989}$　　D) $\frac{1989}{1990}$	2. A
3. 20 ÷ 0.2 = 200 ÷ 2 = 100. A) 0.1　　B) 1　　C) 10　　D) 100	3. D
4. The sum of the measures is 180°; the average is 180°÷3 = 60°. A) 45°　　B) 60°　　C) 90°　　D) 180°	4. B
5. 1 − 0.1 − 0.01 = 1.00 − 0.11 = 0.89. A) 0.98　　B) 0.91　　C) 0.89　　D) 0.8	5. C
6. 5 of the 9 letters are vowels; this is equal to $55\frac{5}{9}\%$. A) 50%　　B) 56%　　C) 63%　　D) 67%	6. B
7. $\sqrt{(1\times9) + (8\times9)} = \sqrt{9 + 72} = \sqrt{81} = 9$. A) 3　　B) 9　　C) 40.5　　D) 81	7. B
8. $3\frac{5}{8} = \frac{3}{1} + \frac{5}{8} = \frac{3 \times 8}{1 \times 8} + \frac{5}{8} = \frac{24}{8} + \frac{5}{8} = \frac{29}{8} = \frac{29 \times 2}{8 \times 2} = \frac{58}{16}$. A) $\frac{29}{16}$　　B) $\frac{34}{16}$　　C) $\frac{58}{16}$　　D) $\frac{53}{16}$	8. C
9. The largest is 22×22×22 = 22×484 = 10 648. A) 2×22×22　B) 22×22×22　C) 22×222　D) 2×2222	9. B
10. Written as a decimal, choice C is equal to 0.11. A) $\frac{1}{9}$　　B) $\frac{10}{11}$　　C) $\frac{11}{100}$　　D) $\frac{1}{11}$	10. C
11. 5÷(5÷5) = 5÷1 = 5. A) 0.2　　B) 1　　C) 5　　D) 25	11. C
12. The reciprocal of 1 is 1 and 1 + 1 = 2. A) 2.5　　B) 2　　C) 1　　D) 0.5	12. C
13. $\frac{3}{2}\times\frac{4}{3}\times\frac{5}{4}\times\frac{6}{5}\times\frac{7}{6}\times\frac{8}{7} = \frac{3\times4\times5\times6\times7\times8}{2\times3\times4\times5\times6\times7} = \frac{1}{2}\times\frac{3}{3}\times\frac{4}{4}\times\frac{5}{5}\times\frac{6}{6}\times\frac{7}{7}\times\frac{8}{1} = \frac{8}{2} = 4$. A) 4　　B) 6　　C) 7　　D) 8	13. A
14. $2^3 + 2^3 = 8 + 8 = 16$. A) 64　　B) 16　　C) 12　　D) 8	14. B
15. 996.47 is between 996 and 997, but it is closer to 996. A) 996　　B) 997　　C) 996.4　　D) 996.5	15. A
16. $0.758 − \frac{3}{4} = 0.758 − 0.750 = 0.008$. A) 0.008　　B) 0.683　　C) 0.75　　D) 0.8	16. A

Go on to the next page ⫸ **7**

		Answers

17. $10 : 100 = (100 \times 10):(100 \times 100) = 1000:10000.$
    A) 10   B) 100   C) 1000   D) 10000
17. D

18. The only primes between 20 and 30 are 23 and 29.
    A) 0 and 10   B) 10 and 20   C) 20 and 30   D) 40 and 50
18. C

19. $(\frac{2}{5} \times \frac{1}{7}) + (\frac{1}{5} \times \frac{2}{7}) = \frac{2}{35} + \frac{2}{35} = \frac{4}{35} = \frac{2 \times 2}{5 \times 7} = \frac{2}{5} \times \frac{2}{7}.$
    A) $\frac{1}{5} \times \frac{1}{7}$ B) $\frac{2}{5} \times \frac{2}{7}$ C) $\frac{3}{5} \times \frac{3}{7}$ D) $\frac{2}{25} \times \frac{2}{49}$
19. B

20. The line segment joining the centers of the 2 circles is equal to 2 radii. Since 2 radii = 1 diameter, the length of a diameter is 12.
    A) 6   B) 12   C) 24   D) 36
20. B

21. $2 \times 3 \times (\frac{1}{2} + \frac{1}{3}) = 6 \times (\frac{3}{6} + \frac{2}{6}) = 6 \times \frac{5}{6} = 5.$
    A) 1   B) 2   C) 5   D) 6
21. C

22. Choice A's numerator is nearly 10 times its denominator.
    A) $\frac{66.7}{6.7}$ B) $\frac{66.7}{67}$ C) $\frac{667}{0.67}$ D) $\frac{667}{6.7}$
22. A

23. Average on 5 tests is 80, so their sum is $5 \times 80 = 400$; average on 4 tests is 86, so their sum is $4 \times 86 = 344$; $400 - 344 = 56.$
    A) 56   B) 62   C) 66   D) 74
23. A

24. 1 m + 1 cm = 1 m + 0.01 m = 1.01 m.
    A) 1.01 m   B) 1.1 m   C) 1.11 m   D) 101 m
24. A

25. The sum of two consecutive whole numbers is always an odd number.
    A) 2   B) 3   C) 5   D) 1989
25. A

26. $1:2.5 = (2 \times 1):(2 \times 2.5) = 2:5 = 40:100 = 40\%.$
    A) 20%   B) $\frac{2}{5}\%$ C) $\frac{5}{2}\%$ D) 40%
26. D

27. The area of the rectangle is $4 \times 9 = 36$. Since the areas of the 3 triangles = the area of the rectangle, their average area is $36 \div 3 = 12.$
    A) 6   B) 8   C) 12   D) 18
27. C

28. $0.123123123 \ldots + 0.231231231 \ldots + 0.312312312 \ldots = 0.666666666 \ldots = \frac{2}{3}.$
    A) 0.66   B) $\frac{6}{10}$ C) $\frac{2}{3}$ D) 0.6666666
28. C

29. Perimeter of this rectangle is 28 cm. The largest possible area that the rectangle could have is if it's a 7 cm by 7 cm square.
    A) 24 cm²   B) 48 cm²   C) 49 cm²   D) 56 cm²
29. C

30. Each ant carries 5×0.001 kg $= 0.005$ kg. The number of ants needed to carry this weight is $2000 \div 0.005 = 400\,000$. A) 10 B) 400 000 C) 4 million D) 10 million	30. B
31. Any prime number greater than 5 is an odd number. If I add 4 to an odd number, I get another odd number. A) is even B) is prime C) ends in 5 D) is odd	31. D
32. $\frac{\pi}{2} > \frac{\pi}{3} > 1 > \frac{\pi}{4} > \frac{\pi}{5}$; so B is smaller than A. C is smaller than B (compare factors). C is larger than D by a factor of $\frac{\pi}{3}$. A) $\frac{\pi}{2} \times \frac{\pi}{3}$ B) $\frac{\pi}{2} \times \frac{\pi}{3} \times \frac{\pi}{4}$ C) $\frac{\pi}{3} \times \frac{\pi}{4} \times \frac{\pi}{5}$ D) $\frac{\pi}{4} \times \frac{\pi}{5}$	32. D
33. Divide by 7. Only $2, 9, 16, 23, 30, 37, \ldots$ leave remainder 2; only $4, 11, 18, \ldots, 74, 81, \ldots$ leave remainder 4. $2 \times 74 = 4 \times 37 = 148$. A) 148 B) 147 C) 146 D) 145	33. A
34. In 9 hours it gained 81 minutes $= 1$ hr. 21 min. After 9 hours, my watch showed 9 A.M. + 9 hours + 1 hr. 21 min. = 7:21 P.M. A) 9:21 P.M. B) 7:21 P.M. C) 6:09 P.M. D) 4:39 P.M.	34. B
35. Since 75% of 240 is 180, the same-sized container of regular yogurt contains 240 calories. A) 135 B) 205 C) 225 D) 240	35. D
36. 6 cassettes cost the same as 4 CD's. If I buy 3 CD's and 6 cassettes for \$84, then 7 CD's also cost \$84. So 1 CD costs \$12. A) \$10 B) \$11 C) \$12 D) \$13	36. C
37. Any multiple of $2 \times 3 \times 5 = 30$ will be divisible by 6, 10, and 15, but not by 14. A) 6 B) 10 C) 14 D) 15	37. C
38. At 3:30, the hands are at 17.5 min. and 30 min.; 12.5 min. = 75°. A) 90° B) 75° C) 65° D) 60°	38. B
39. Each person shakes hands with 30 others. It seems that 30×31 handshakes occur. This counts each shake *twice*, so divide by 2. A) 15×31 B) 30×30 C) 30×31 D) 31×31	39. A
40. The diagonal is $13 + 10 + 6 + 9 = 38$; add 3 to 2nd row to get $8 + 10 + 17 + 3 = 38$. Upper right-hand corner must now equal 14, so the top row needs a 7 between the 13 and the 4. Finally, $7 + 10 + 5 + x = 38$, so $x = 16$. A) 14 B) 15 C) 16 D) 18	40. C

Table for problem 40:

13		4	
8	10	17	
	5	6	12
	x		9

The end of the contest 🖎 **7**

Solutions

1989-90 Annual 7th Grade Contest

7

Tuesday, February 6, 1990

Contest Information

■ **Solutions** Turn the page for detailed contest solutions (written in the question boxes) and letter answers (in the answer columns on the right).

■ **Scores** When reviewing these questions, remember *this is a contest, not a test.* There is no "passing" or "failing" score. Few students score as high as 30 points (75% correct); students with even half that, 15 points, *deserve commendation!*

■ **Answers & Rating Scale** Turn to page 153 for the letter answers to each question and the rating scale for this contest.

1. $5 \times 1¢ + 5 \times 5¢ + 5 \times 10¢ = 5¢ + 25¢ + 50¢ = 80¢.$ A) 15¢ B) 60¢ C) 70¢ D) 80¢	1. D
2. $1990 = 199 \times 10$, so choice B is correct. A) 0 B) 10 C) 100 D) 1000	2. B
3. Today, Uncle Joe is 68 years old. Fifty years ago, he was 18 years old, or 50 years younger. A) 18 years B) 40 years C) 50 years D) 68 years	3. C
4. $\frac{1}{5} + \frac{2}{10} + \frac{3}{15} + \frac{4}{20} = \frac{1}{5} + \frac{1}{5} + \frac{1}{5} + \frac{1}{5} = \frac{4}{5}.$ A) $\frac{4}{5}$ B) 1 C) $1\frac{1}{5}$ D) $1\frac{2}{5}$	4. A
5. $0.1 = 0.1000$ and this is greater than the other choices. A) 0.0099 B) 0.02 C) 0.0111 D) 0.1	5. D
6. $10 + 10 + 10 + 10 + 10 + 10 + 10 + 10 + 10 = 90$ $= 10 \times 10 - 10.$ A) 0 B) 1 C) 9 D) 10	6. D
7. The only prime number which is divisible by 3 is 3; there is 1. A) 0 B) 1 C) 3 D) 9	7. B
8. $1.11 - 0.999 = 1.110 - 0.999 = 0.111.$ A) 0.111 B) 0.888 C) 1.111 D) 2.109	8. A
9. Boatman can travel in his Boatmobile at 80 km/hr. In 1 hour he can travel 80 km, so in 30 minutes he travels 40 km. A) $\frac{1}{2}$ minute B) 30 minutes C) 40 minutes D) 2 hours	9. B
10. $4 \times 6 \times 8 \times 10 = (2 \times 2) \times (3 \times 2) \times (4 \times 2) \times (5 \times 2) = (2 \times 3 \times 4 \times 5) \times 16.$ A) 2 B) 6 C) 8 D) 16	10. D
11. This will be a rhombus whenever a pair of adjacent sides is equal. A) $AB = CD$ B) $AB = BA$ C) $AB = AD$ D) $BC = AD$	11. C
12. Since $\frac{2}{3} \div \frac{4}{3} = \frac{2}{3} \times \frac{3}{4} = \frac{1}{2}, \frac{2}{3} = \frac{1}{2} \times \frac{4}{3}.$ A) $\frac{1}{2}$ B) $\frac{2}{3}$ C) $\frac{4}{3}$ D) 2	12. A
13. $3 + 2 \times 3 + 3 = 3 + 6 + 3 = 12$, so choice A is correct. A) $3+2\times3+3$ B) $2+3\times2+2$ C) $1+3\times1+2$ D) $1+3\times3\times1$	13. A
14. $4 \div \frac{1}{4} = 4 \times 4 = 16.$ A) $\frac{1}{16}$ B) 1 C) $\frac{17}{4}$ D) 16	14. D
15. The largest two-digit number is 99, so the largest possible value of the three-digit number is $99 + 50 = 149$. A) 149 B) 150 C) 151 D) 999	15. A

Go on to the next page ▐▐▐➡ **7**

16. $0.02 \times 0.05 = 0.0010 = 0.001$, so choice C is correct. A) 0.1 B) 0.01 C) 0.001 D) 0.0001	16. C
17. Acute angles$+90°=$angle total$=180°$; so acute angles total $90°$. A) $60°$ B) $90°$ C) $120°$ D) $180°$	17. B
18. 0.0049 is between 0.00 and 0.01; it is closer to 0.00. A) 0.00 B) 0.004 C) 0.005 D) 0.01	18. A
19. $1234 - (1 + 10 + 100 + 1000) = 1234 - 1111$. A) 111 B) 123 C) 234 D) 1111	19. D
20. 50% of $\frac{1}{50} = \frac{50}{100} \times \frac{1}{50} = \frac{1}{2} \times \frac{1}{50} = \frac{1}{100} = 0.01$. A) 0.01 B) 1 C) 0.25 D) 0.04	20. A
21. $(0.1 \times 0.2 \times 0.3) - (\frac{1}{10} \times \frac{2}{10} \times \frac{3}{10}) = (0.1 \times 0.2 \times 0.3) - (0.1 \times 0.2 \times 0.3) = 0$. A) 0 B) 1 C) 0.246 D) 0.594	21. A
22. If twice the length of a diameter of a circle is 24, the length of a diameter is 12 and the length of a radius is 6. A) 12 B) 6 C) 3 D) 1	22. B
23. $\frac{1}{10} + \frac{1}{5} + \frac{1}{10} + \frac{1}{5} + \frac{1}{10} + \frac{1}{5} + \frac{1}{10} + \frac{1}{5} = (4 \times \frac{1}{10}) + (4 \times \frac{1}{5}) = \frac{2}{5} + \frac{4}{5} = \frac{6}{5}$. A) $\frac{7}{10}$ B) $\frac{4}{5}$ C) 1 D) $\frac{6}{5}$	23. D
24. $(37 + 41) \div 2 = 78 \div 2 = 39$. A) 37 B) 38 C) 39 D) 40	24. C
25. $22:44 = (2 \times 11):(4 \times 11) = 2:4 = 1:2 = (1 \times 44):(2 \times 44) = 44:88$. A) 44:22 B) 33:55 C) 11:33 D) 44:88	25. D
26. Since the perimeter of each triangle is 24, each side is $24 \div 3 = 8$. Since quadrilateral *ABCD* has 4 sides, its perimeter is $4 \times 8 = 32$. A) 24 B) 32 C) 40 D) 48	26. B
27. $\sqrt{1} + \sqrt{4} + \sqrt{9} + \sqrt{16} = 1 + 2 + 3 + 4 = 10 = \sqrt{100}$. A) 10 B) 25 C) 30 D) 100	27. D
28. 60 minutes before is 9:56 A.M.; 1 minute later is 9:57 P.M. A) 11:57 A.M. B) 9:59 A.M. C) 9:57 A.M. D) 10:01 A.M.	28. C
29. $10^2 - 1 = 100 - 1 = 99 = 9 \times 11$. A) 9×9 B) 9×10 C) 9×11 D) 19	29. C
30. 1 km $= 1000$ m $= (1000 \times 100)$ cm $= 100\,000$ cm $= 10^5$ cm. A) 10^6 cm B) 10^5 cm C) 10^4 cm D) 10^3 cm	30. B

31. The number of years = (140 million)÷(700 thousand) = (140 000 000)÷(700 000) = 1400÷7 = 200. A) 2 years B) 20 years C) 200 years D) 2000 years	31. C
32. $3^2+4^2+3^2+4^2+3^2+4^2+3^2+4^2 = (9\times4) + (16\times4) = 36 + 64 = 100.$ A) 10^2 B) 14^2 C) 20^2 D) 28^2	32. A
33. Since $\frac{2}{3}$ of 1001 = $667\frac{1}{3}$, the least number of votes that a candidate would need to win this election is 668. A) 601 B) 666 C) 667 D) 668	33. D
34. The sum of seven consecutive whole numbers is 77. The middle number is 77÷7 = 11, so the largest number is 11 + 3 = 14. A) 7 B) 11 C) 14 D) 17	34. C
35. Using the Pythagorean Theorem, the square of the length of the unknown leg is 20 − 16 = 4. Since this is the square of the length of the unknown leg, the length of the leg is $\sqrt{4}$ = 2. A) 2 B) 4 C) 6 D) 36	35. A
36. 3.5:560 = 7:1120 = 1:160 = 4:640; this truck would use 4 tanks of gas to drive 640 km. A) 4 B) 4.5 C) 6 D) 11.5	36. A
37. $\S(1)\S = \frac{1}{1+1} = \frac{1}{2}$; $\S(\S(1)\S)\S = \S(\frac{1}{2})\S = \dfrac{\frac{1}{2}}{\frac{1}{2}+1} = \frac{1}{2}\div\frac{3}{2} = \frac{1}{2}\times\frac{2}{3} = \frac{1}{3}.$ A) $\frac{1}{2}$ B) $\frac{1}{3}$ C) $\frac{1}{4}$ D) $\frac{2}{3}$	37. B
38. John's age is $\frac{2}{5} = \frac{8}{20}$ of Pat's age, but $\frac{3}{4} = \frac{15}{20}$ of Mary's age. The ratio of Pat's age to Mary's age is $\frac{15}{20}:\frac{8}{20}$ = 15:8. A) 3:15 B) 8:15 C) 15:8 D) 10:3	38. C
39. Since 8 divides 360, 8 divides the number. (If 8 divides the last 3 digits of a whole number, it divides the whole number.) A) 9 B) 8 C) 6 D) 3	39. B
40. When the product of the first 1001 positive primes is divided by the product of the first 1000 positive primes, the quotient is the 1001st prime. A) 1000 B) 1001 C) prime D) even	40. C

The end of the contest ✍ **7**

Solutions

1990-91 Annual 7th Grade Contest
Tuesday, February 5, 1991

7

Contest Information

- **Solutions** Turn the page for detailed contest solutions (written in the question boxes) and letter answers (in the answer columns on the right).

- **Scores** When reviewing these questions, remember *this is a contest, not a test.* There is no "passing" or "failing" score. Few students score as high as 30 points (75% correct); students with even half that, 15 points, *deserve commendation!*

- **Answers & Rating Scale** Turn to page 154 for the letter answers to each question and the rating scale for this contest.

1. Order of multiplication doesn't matter, so $19 \times 91 = 91 \times 19$. A) 9 B) 19 C) 91 D) 1991	1. B
2. 1 fortnight = 2 weeks = 2×7 days = 14 days. A) 4 B) 7 C) 8 D) 14	2. D
3. $\frac{1}{1} + \frac{22}{22} + \frac{333}{333} = 1 + 1 + 1 = 3$. A) 1 B) 3 C) 6 D) 356	3. B
4. Ice cream pops cost 75¢ each, so 4 pops cost \$3. Two cones, at 95¢ each cost \$1.90. The total cost is \$4.90. A) \$1.20 B) \$3.00 C) \$4.90 D) \$6.00	4. C
5. $100 - 99.4 = 0.6$, but $99.4 - 99 = 0.4$; so 99.4 is closest to 99. A) 99 B) 100 C) 101 D) 102	5. A
6. $\sqrt{1 \times 9 \times 9 \times 1} = \sqrt{81} = 9$. A) 3 B) 9 C) 81 D) 1991	6. B
7. In one hour, the minute hand of a circular clock moves *once* around the clock − so the answer is 360°. A) 1° B) 60° C) 120° D) 360°	7. D
8. $1^1 \times 1^2 \times 1^3 \times \ldots \times 1^{100} = 1 \times 1 \times 1 \times \ldots \times 1 = 1$. A) 0 B) 1 C) 10 D) 100	8. B
9. If the perimeter of an equilateral triangle is 36, the length of each side is one-third of 36, so the length of each side is 12. A) 6 B) 12 C) 18 D) 36	9. B
10. $3.141 \div 0.9 = 3.49$ (most easily verified on a calculator). A) $\pi \div 0.9$ B) 3.39 C) 3.49 D) 3.59	10. C
11. The sum is $1 + 2 + 4 + 8 + 16 + 32 = 63$. A) 30 B) 31 C) 32 D) 63	11. D
12. 1000×0.0001 = one thousand $\times$ one ten-thousandth = 0.1. A) 1 B) 0.1 C) 0.01 D) 0.001	12. B
13. $\frac{5 \times 4 \times 3 \times 2 \times 1}{1 \times 2 \times 3 \times 4 \times 5} = \frac{1 \times 2 \times 3 \times 4 \times 5}{1 \times 2 \times 3 \times 4 \times 5} = 1$. A) 1 B) 5 C) 24 D) 120	13. A
14. $0.1 + 0.2 + 0.3 + 0.4 = 1.0 = 100\%$. A) 1% B) 10% C) 100% D) 1000%	14. C
15. There are 100 centimeters in 1 meter, so 1 cm = 0.01 m. A) 100 m B) 10 m C) 0.1 m D) 0.01 m	15. D

Go on to the next page ⅢⅢ➡ **7**

16. $\frac{46 \times 4}{23 \times 2} = 2 \times 2 = 4.$ A) 2 B) 4 C) 23 D) 46	16. B
17. \$1 U.S. = 80¢ + 20¢ = \$1 Canadian + \$(1/4) Canadian. A) \$1.25 B) \$1.20 C) 80¢ D) 75¢	17. A
18. Since 10/11 = 30/33, the first inequality is false. A) $\frac{10}{11} < \frac{29}{33}$ B) $\frac{4}{5} < \frac{25}{30}$ C) $\frac{3}{7} < \frac{16}{35}$ D) $\frac{7}{13} < \frac{22}{39}$	18. A
19. The average is (1+2+3+4+5+6+7+8+9+10)/10 = 55/10. A) 5 B) 5.5 C) 6 D) 10	19. B
20. $\frac{3}{4}\%$ is slightly less than 1% and equals (3/4)(1/100). A) 0.75 B) 0.075 C) 0.0075 D) 0.00075	20. C
21. $10 \times 0.1 \times 10 \times 0.1 \times 10 \times 0.1 = 1 \times 1 \times 1 = 1.$ A) 0 B) 0.1 C) 1 D) 10	21. C
22. In a recipe, the ratio of eggs to sugar is 2 eggs per 25 g of sugar. For 175 g of sugar, we need $7 \times 2 = 14$ eggs. A) 12 B) 13 C) 14 D) 15	22. C
23. $(\frac{1}{2} \times \frac{1}{3}) \div (\frac{1}{2} - \frac{1}{3}) = \frac{1}{6} \div \frac{1}{6} = 1.$ A) $\frac{1}{6}$ B) $\frac{1}{5}$ C) $\frac{1}{2}$ D) 1	23. D
24. The sum of the reciprocals of the four whole number factors of 6 is 1/1 + 1/2 + 1/3 + 1/6 = 2. A) 2 B) 12 C) 1/12 D) 7/6	24. A
25. $12^3 = (2 \times 2 \times 3)^3 = (2 \times 2 \times 3) \times (2 \times 2 \times 3) \times (2 \times 2 \times 3) = 2^6 \times 3^3.$ A) $2^8 \times 3^3$ B) $2^6 \times 3^3$ C) $2^4 \times 3^2$ D) $2^2 \times 3^2$	25. B
26. The product is $2 \times 3 \times 5 \times 7 = 210.$ [Note: 1 is *not* prime.] A) 24 B) 30 C) 95 D) 210	26. D
27. $1 + 2 + 3 + 4 + 5 + 6 + 7 + 8 = 36 = 6^2.$ A) 6 B) $\sqrt{6}$ C) $\sqrt{81}$ D) 6^2	27. D
28. If the time now is 2:17 P.M., then 12 hours from now will be 2:17 A.M., and 1 minute before that will be 2:16 A.M. A) 1:17 A.M. B) 2:15 A.M. C) 2:16 A.M. D) 2:18 A.M.	28. C
29. Work backwards. The reciprocal of 10 is 1/10. The reciprocal of 1/10 is 10. A) 10 B) 100 C) $\frac{1}{10}$ D) $\frac{1}{100}$	29. A

Go on to the next page ▪▪▶ 7

30. If boys:girls is 3:1, there are at least 2 more boys than girls. If 2 boys leave, there *cannot* be more girls than boys remaining. A) 2:1 B) 1:1 C) 5:2 D) 1:2	30. D
31. The measure of the complement of $\angle A$ is 30°, so $m\angle A = 60°$; and the measure of the supplement of $\angle A$ is 120°. A) 30° B) 60° C) 120° D) 150°	31. C
32. Since $\frac{2}{3}$ is $\frac{1}{2}$, $\frac{1}{3}$ is $\frac{1}{4}$ and $\frac{3}{3}$ is $\frac{3}{4}$; so the number is $\frac{3}{4}$. A) $\frac{3}{4}$ B) $\frac{1}{3}$ C) $\frac{3}{2}$ D) 3	32. A
33. If a car is traveling at 60 km per hour, it travels 1 km each minute, so in 72 minutes it travels 72 km. A) 72 km B) 132 km C) 144 km D) 4320 km	33. A
34. The only positive number whose square is its double is 2, since 2^2 is equal to $2 \times 2 = 4$. A) 4 B) 3 C) 2 D) 1	34. C
35. If a triangle with base 10 has the same area as a square with side 5, the area of the triangle is $5 \times 5 = 25$. A triangle with base 10 and altitude 5 has area 25. A) 2.5 B) 5 C) 10 D) 25	35. B
36. Between 1 and 1991, the whole numbers that are multiples of 5 *and* are even are 10, 20, 30, . . . , 1980, 1990. A) 400 B) 399 C) 398 D) 199	36. D
37. $1\frac{1}{2} \times 1\frac{1}{3} \times 1\frac{1}{4} \times 1\frac{1}{5} \times 1\frac{1}{6} = \frac{3}{2} \times \frac{4}{3} \times \frac{5}{4} \times \frac{6}{5} \times \frac{7}{6} = \frac{7}{2}$. A) $1\frac{1}{720}$ B) $2\frac{1}{2}$ C) 3 D) $3\frac{1}{2}$	37. D
38. 1991^2 ends in a "1" and is just less than $2000^2 = 4$ million. A) 2 054 081 B) 3 054 083 C) 3 964 081 D) 4 054 081	38. C
39. The angles of a quadrilateral add up to 360°. To be in the ratio 1:2:3:4, they must be 36°, 72°, 108°, and 144°. A) 18° B) 30° C) 36° D) 72°	39. C
40. The ones' digits are 3, 9, 7, 1, 3, 9, 7, 1, ... The 1991st digit is 7. A) 1 B) 3 C) 7 D) 9	40. C

The end of the contest 🖅 **7**

Solutions

1982-83 Annual 8th Grade Contest
Tuesday, February 8, 1983

8

Contest Information

- **Solutions** Turn the page for detailed contest solutions (written in the question boxes) and letter answers (in the answer columns on the right).

- **Scores** When reviewing these questions, remember *this is a contest, not a test.* There is no "passing" or "failing" score. Few students score as high as 30 points (75% correct); students with even half that, 15 points, *deserve commendation!*

- **Answers & Rating Scale** Turn to page 155 for the letter answers to each question and the rating scale for this contest.

1. $10\,001 \times 1983 = (10\,000 \times 1983) + (1 \times 1983) = 19\,831\,983.$ A) $21\,813$ B) $200\,283$ C) $1\,984\,983$ D) $19\,831\,983$	1. D
2. $\sqrt{36} + \sqrt{64} = 6 + 8 = 14 = \sqrt{196}.$ A) $\sqrt{10}$ B) $\sqrt{14}$ C) $\sqrt{100}$ D) $\sqrt{196}$	2. D
3. The sum of the angle measures in a triangle is $180°$ and in a square is $360°$. The ratio is $180{:}360 = 1{:}2$. A) $1{:}2$ B) $2{:}3$ C) $3{:}4$ D) $4{:}3$	3. A
4. There are 28 days; 28 days $\times$ 24 hours per day $= 672$ hours. A) 196 B) 696 C) 672 D) 720	4. C
5. $\frac{1982}{1983} \times \frac{1983}{1984} = \frac{1982}{1984} = \frac{991}{992}$ A) 1 B) $\frac{1}{2}$ C) $\frac{991}{992}$ D) $\frac{1982}{1983}$	5. C
6. $120\% = \frac{120}{100} = \frac{12}{10} = \frac{6}{5}$, so choice C is correct. A) $\frac{4}{5}$ B) $\frac{5}{4}$ C) $\frac{6}{5}$ D) 120	6. C
7. By the Pythagorean Theorem, the third side is 5; perimeter is $3 + 4 + 5 = 12$. A) 5 B) 6 C) 7 D) 12	7. D
8. $(-1) \times (-1) \times (-1) = 1 \times (-1) = -1.$ A) -1 B) 1 C) -3 D) 3	8. A
9. Since the hundredths' digit is 5, round up to 87.6 A) 90 B) 88 C) 87.5 D) 87.6	9. D
10. The even perfect squares between 10 and 70 are 16, 36, and 64, so choice D is correct. A) 4 B) 25 C) 52 D) 64	10. D
11. $\frac{3}{4}$ divided by $\frac{1}{2}$ equals $\frac{3}{4} \times 2 = \frac{6}{4} = \frac{3}{2}$. A) $\frac{4}{6}$ B) $\frac{3}{2}$ C) $\frac{1}{24}$ D) $\frac{3}{8}$	11. B
12. The product is $\geq 100 \times 100 = 10\,000$ and $< 1000 \times 1000 = 1\,000\,000$. The product may have either 5 or 6 digits. A) 3 digits B) 5 digits C) 7 digits D) 9 digits	12. B
13. $2^6 + 2^6 = 64 + 64 = 128 = 2^7.$ A) 4^6 B) 4^{12} C) 4^{36} D) 2^7	13. D
14. The smallest one-digit prime is 2; the smallest two-digit prime is 11. Their product is $2 \times 11 = 22$. A) 18 B) 22 C) 26 D) 33	14. B
15. A negative number is less than either 0 or a positive number. A) -1000 B) $1/100$ C) 0 D) $1/1000$	15. A

Go on to the next page ⏵ **8**

16. $\frac{1}{4} - \frac{1}{2} = \frac{1}{4} - \frac{2}{4} = -\frac{1}{4}$.

   A) $\frac{1}{2}$ B) $\frac{1}{4}$ C) $-\frac{1}{2}$ D) $-\frac{1}{4}$

16.

D

17. If 1 liter of syrup is mixed with 4 liters of water, there is a total of 5 liters, The part that is syrup is 1/5 = 20%.

   A) 25%   B) 20%   C) $\frac{1}{4}$%   D) $\frac{1}{5}$%

17.

B

18. The shaded triangle has a base of 8 and a height of 4. Its area is ½×8×4 = 16.

   A) 16   B) 24   C) 32   D) 64

18.

A

19. $3^2 + 4^2 + 12^2 = 9 + 16 + 144 = 169 = 13^2$.

   A) 13^2 B) 15^2 C) 17^2 D) 19^2

19.

A

20. The fewest possible coins he could have would be 1 half-dollar, 1 quarter, 2 dimes, and 4 pennies.

   A) 0   B) 1   C) 2   D) 3

20.

A

21. $\frac{2}{0.5} + \frac{5}{0.2} = \frac{20}{5} + \frac{50}{2} = 4 + 25 = 29$.

   A) 29   B) $2\frac{1}{2}$ C) 1   D) $\frac{7}{10}$

21.

A

22. $\frac{-1}{100} = -0.01$; this differs from 0.01 by *only* 0.02.

   A) −0.10   B) 0.01   C) −0.04   D) 0.10

22.

B

23. The dimensions of the rectangle are 3 diameters by 2 diameters or 24 by 16. The area is 24×16 = 384.

   A) 48   B) 96   C) 192   D) 384

23.

D

24. Since $\frac{1}{12} = \frac{1}{4} \times \frac{1}{3}$, $\frac{1}{12}$ is $\frac{1}{4}$ of $\frac{1}{3}$ or 25% of $\frac{1}{3}$.

   A) $\frac{1}{4}$%   B) 25%   C) 75%   D) 400%

24.

B

25. The least common multiple of 4, 6, and 8 is 24; all three events occur on the same day every 24 days. If all three events occur on July 1, they will next all occur together on July 25.

   A) July 9   B) July 19   C) July 24   D) July 25

25.

D

26. The complement of 60° is 30°; the supplement of 30° is 150°.

   A) 30°   B) 60°   C) 90°   D) 150°

26.

D

27. If the average of five consecutive even numbers is 50, the middle one is 50 and the others are 46, 48, 52, and 54.

   A) 42   B) 44   C) 46   D) 48

27.

C

28. The average of $\frac{2}{3}$ and $\frac{5}{6}$ is $(\frac{2}{3}+\frac{5}{6})\div2 = \frac{9}{6}\times\frac{1}{2} = \frac{9}{12} = \frac{3}{4}$.

   A) $\frac{7}{36}$ B) $\frac{3}{4}$ C) $\frac{4}{3}$ D) $\frac{7}{18}$

28.

B

Go on to the next page ⇒ **8**

111

29.	$1/2 - 1/3 = 1/6$, so 20 people is one-sixth of the full room. The full room contains $6 \times 20 = 120$ people. A) 60 people B) 80 people C) 90 people D) 120 people	29. D
30.	$\sqrt{8 + \sqrt{64}} = \sqrt{8 + 8} = \sqrt{16} = 4$. A) 4 B) 8 C) 16 D) 64	30. A
31.	Divide by 7: 2 *whosits* equals 5 *whatsits*. Now multiply by 10. A) 125 *whosits* B) 70 *whosits* C) 20 *whosits* D) 7 *whosits*	31. C
32.	Substitute 50 for n in the formula: $\frac{50(50+1)}{2} = 25 \times 51$. The correct answer is choice A. A) 25×51 B) 50×51 C) 25×50 D) 50×50	32. A
33.	$\frac{1}{8} + \frac{3}{8} = \frac{4}{8} = \frac{1}{2} = \frac{3\frac{1}{2}}{7} = \frac{1}{7} + \frac{2\frac{1}{2}}{7}$, so choice C is correct. A) 3 B) 4 C) 2½ D) 3½	33. C
34.	The baseball team plays $75 + 45 = 120$ games in all. Since 60% of 120 is 72 and the team has already won 50, it needs to win $72 - 50 = 22$ games to have a 60% win record for the season. A) 20 games B) 27 games C) 22 games D) 30 games	34. C
35.	Turn the diagram upside down. The shaded area is a triangle with base 2 and height 3. Its area is $\frac{1}{2} \times 2 \times 3 = 3$. A) 2 sq. units B) 3 sq. units C) 5 sq. units D) 6 sq. units	35. B
36.	$x = -1$, $y = \frac{1}{2}$, and z is approximately 1.25. The reciprocals are $-1, 2, 0.8$ for a sum of 1.8. A) -3.6 B) 0.2 C) 1 D) 1.8	36. D
37.	$\sqrt{999999} < \sqrt{1000000} = 1000$; desired root is slightly less. A) 3 B) 5 C) 7 D) 9	37. D
38.	The curved path is 3 semicircles, each with a diameter of $42 \div 3 = 14$. Circumference of semi-circle is $\frac{1}{2} \times \pi \times 14 = 7\pi$; 3 semicircles $= 21\pi$. A) 14π B) 21π C) 28π D) 42π	38. B
39.	If the pilot flew the 1st part of the trip at full speed, it would have taken him only 2 minutes. The entire trip at full speed takes 6 minutes. 80 km in 6 minutes = 800 km in 60 minutes. A) 400 km/hr B) 600 km/hr C) 800 km/hr D) 1000 km/hr	39. C
40.	The only small cube with exactly two painted faces is the middle one of each edge. Since a cube has 12 edges, there are 12 small cubes with exactly two painted faces. A) 18 B) 12 C) 9 D) 8	40. B

The end of the contest ✍ **8**

Solutions

1983-84 Annual 8th Grade Contest

Tuesday, February 14, 1984

8

Contest Information

- **Solutions** Turn the page for detailed contest solutions (written in the question boxes) and letter answers (in the answer columns on the right).

- **Scores** When reviewing these questions, remember *this is a contest, not a test*. There is no "passing" or "failing" score. Few students score as high as 30 points (75% correct); students with even half that, 15 points, *deserve commendation!*

- **Answers & Rating Scale** Turn to page 156 for the letter answers to each question and the rating scale for this contest.

1.	$\dfrac{1984 \times 1984}{1984} = \dfrac{1984}{1984} \times \dfrac{1984}{1} = 1 \times 1984 = 1984.$	1.
	A) 1 B) 2 C) 4 D) 1984	D
2.	$333^2 = 333 \times 333 > 90000$; the ones' digit of the product is 9. A) 666 B) 999 C) 110889 D) 333333	2. C
3.	A quadrilateral is a 4-sided polygon; a rhombus has 4 sides. A) rhombus B) pentagon C) hexagon D) sphere	3. A
4.	$4\frac{3}{4} - 3\frac{7}{8} = 4\frac{6}{8} - 3\frac{7}{8} = 3\frac{14}{8} - 3\frac{7}{8} = -1.$ A) $1\frac{1}{2}$ B) $1\frac{3}{4}$ C) $1\frac{7}{8}$ D) $\frac{7}{8}$	4. D
5.	$(0.3)(0.3) = 0.09 = \frac{9}{100}.$ A) $\frac{1}{3}$ B) $\frac{3}{100}$ C) $\frac{90}{100}$ D) $\frac{9}{100}$	5. D
6.	$\frac{1-2}{2-1} = \frac{-1}{1} = -1.$ A) 1 B) $\frac{1}{2}$ C) 0 D) -1	6. D
7.	$77000000 = 7 \times 11 \times 1000000$; the prime factors are 2, 5, 7, & 11. A) 3 B) 5 C) 7 D) 11	7. D
8.	$(\frac{4}{3} + \frac{10}{9} + \frac{28}{27}) - (\frac{1}{3} + \frac{1}{9} + \frac{1}{27}) = (1\frac{1}{3} + 1\frac{1}{9} + 1\frac{1}{27}) - (\frac{1}{3} + \frac{1}{9} + \frac{1}{27}) = 3.$ A) 0 B) 1 C) 2 D) 3	8. D
9.	Greatest common divisor of positive evens which differ by 2 is 2. A) 1 B) 2 C) 4 D) 8	9. B
10.	$0.888 + 0.222 = 1.110$, so choice C is correct. A) 1.000 B) 1.010 C) 1.110 D) 1.111	10. C
11.	The measure of one angle of an isosceles triangle is 120°. The sum of the measures of the other angles is 60°; each is 30°. A) 30° B) 40° C) 60° D) 120°	11. A
12.	0 has no reciprocal; the reciprocals of $\frac{1}{2}, \frac{2}{3}$, and 1 are 2, $\frac{3}{2}$, and 1. A) 0 B) $\frac{1}{2}$ C) $\frac{2}{3}$ D) 1	12. D
13.	$\dfrac{5 \times 10 \times 15 \times 20}{5 \times 5 \times 5 \times 5} = \frac{5}{5} \times \frac{10}{5} \times \frac{15}{5} \times \frac{20}{5} = 1 \times 2 \times 3 \times 4 = 24.$ A) 10 B) 12 C) 24 D) 750	13. C
14.	(10% of 20) - (20% of 10) = $0.1 \times 20 - 0.2 \times 10 = 2 - 2 = 0.$ A) 2 B) $\frac{1}{2}$ C) 1 D) 0	14. D
15.	If the product of two whole numbers is 36, their greatest possible sum occurs when the numbers are 1 and 36. The sum is 37. A) 12 B) 13 C) 20 D) 37	15. D

16. If the sum of two whole numbers is 36, their greatest possible product occurs when they both equal 18. Their product is 324. A) 35 B) 260 C) 320 D) 324	16. D

17. $62\frac{1}{2}\% = 62.5\% = \frac{625}{1000} = \frac{25}{40} = \frac{5}{8}.$

A) $\frac{3}{5}$ B) $\frac{5}{8}$ C) $\frac{5}{6}$ D) $\frac{2}{3}$

17.
B

18. Since $AB = 8$ and $AB{:}BC = 2{:}5 = 8{:}20$, $BC = 20$ and $AC = 8+20 = 28$.

A) 20   B) 24   C) 28   D) 40

18.
C

19. The greatest possible sum is $9+9+9+9+9 = 45$.

A) 1   B) 37   C) 44   D) 50

19.
D

20. The average of $\frac{1}{5}$ and $\frac{1}{7}$ is $(\frac{1}{5} + \frac{1}{7}) \div 2 = (\frac{7}{35} + \frac{5}{35}) \div 2 = \frac{12}{35} \div 2 = \frac{6}{35}$.

A) $\frac{12}{35}$ B) $\frac{1}{6}$ C) $\frac{1}{12}$ D) $\frac{6}{35}$

20.
D

21. Perimeter is twice the sum of the lengths of 2 adjacent sides. The sum of the lengths of these adjacent sides is $\frac{1}{9} \times \frac{1}{2} = \frac{1}{18}$.

A) $\frac{1}{36}$ B) $\frac{1}{18}$ C) $\frac{2}{3}$ D) $\frac{2}{9}$

21.
B

22. 125% of $16 = 1.25 \times 16 = 20 = 20\%$ of 100.

A) 20   B) 80   C) 100   D) 120

22.
C

23. The polygon with the fewest number of sides is a triangle.

A) 2   B) 3   C) 4   D) 5

23.
B

24. If 75% of a number is 36, then 150% of it is $2 \times 36 = 72$.

A) 18   B) 48   C) 54   D) 72

24.
D

25. $\dfrac{1 - \frac{1}{2}}{1 + \frac{1}{2}} = \dfrac{\frac{1}{2}}{\frac{3}{2}} = \frac{1}{2} \times \frac{2}{3} = \frac{1}{3}.$

A) 6   B) 3   C) $\frac{1}{2}$ D) $\frac{1}{3}$

25.

D

26. $\angle BCD = \angle BCA + \angle ACD = 60° + 90°$

The measure of angle BCD is $150°$.

A) $30°$ B) $60°$ C) $90°$ D) $150°$

26.

D

27. Interest for a year is 12% of $\$800 = \$96$. Since 9 months is three-fourths of a year, 9 months' interest is $\frac{3}{4} \times \$96 = \$72$.

A) $\$24$ B) $\$48$ C) $\$72$ D) $\$96$

27.
C

28. The sailboat's distance from its starting point is found by the Pythagorean Theorem. $6^2 + 8^2 = 10^2$, so its distance is 10 km.

A) 10 km   B) 12 km   C) 14 km   D) 48 km

28.
A

Go on to the next page ⫸ **8**

29. $100\% - 99\frac{44}{100}\% = \frac{56}{100}\% = \frac{14}{25}\%$, so choice C is correct. A) $\frac{16}{25}\%$ B) $\frac{33}{50}\%$ C) $\frac{14}{25}\%$ D) $1\frac{44}{100}\%$	29. C
30. The area of the rectangle is 60 sq. m.; its perimeter is 32 m. The side of a square having this perimeter is 8; its area is 64 sq m. A) 165 sq. m B) 56 sq. m C) 8 sq. m D) 4 sq. m	30. D
31. 24 km in 36 minutes = 2 km in 3 minutes = 40 km in 60 minutes, so choice D is correct. A) 60 B) 48 C) 45 D) 40	31. D
32. Pair 1 & 100, 2 & 99, 3 & 98, etc. Each has an average of $50\frac{1}{2}$. A) 49 B) $49\frac{1}{2}$ C) 50 D) $50\frac{1}{2}$	32. D
33. $2^5 = 32$; $3^3 = 27$; $5^2 = 25$; and $2^2 \times 7 = 28$. $(32+27+25) \div 3 = 28$. A) 2^5 B) 3^3 C) 5^2 D) $2^2 \times 7$	33. D
34. If $a \blacklozenge b$ means $(a \times b) + b$, then $2 \blacklozenge 3 = (2 \times 3) + 3 = 9$. A) 12 B) 9 C) 8 D) 6	34. B
35. The increasing numbers between 5000 and 10000 are: 5678, 5679, 5689, 5789, and 6789. There are 5 in all. A) 3 B) 4 C) 5 D) 6	35. C
36. If $3x = 21$, then $7 \times 3x = 7 \times 21$ or $21x = 147$. A) 3 B) 7 C) 63 D) 147	36. D
37. In decreasing order, the numbers are: 332, 331, 323, 322, 321, 313, 312, 233, 232, 231, 223, 221, 213, 212, 133, 132, 123, and 122. A) 12 B) 16 C) 18 D) 20	37. C
38. $\frac{2}{3} = 0.666...$, $\frac{3}{4} = 0.75$, $\frac{5}{8} = 0.625$, and $\frac{5}{7} = 0.7142857142857...$, so choice C is correct. A) $\frac{5}{8}, \frac{5}{7}, \frac{3}{4}, \frac{2}{3}$ B) $\frac{5}{7}, \frac{3}{4}, \frac{2}{3}, \frac{5}{8}$ C) $\frac{3}{4}, \frac{5}{7}, \frac{2}{3}, \frac{5}{8}$ D) $\frac{2}{3}, \frac{5}{7}, \frac{3}{4}, \frac{5}{8}$	38. C
39. The path consists of 4 line segments and 4 quarter- circles of radius 1 cm. The area this bounds is the area of 1 circle and the 5 squares shown. Total area = $\pi + 5$. Using $\pi = 3.14$, area = 8.14. A) 7 B) 8 C) 9 D) 10	39. B
40. Sides of small right △ are proportional to sides of the large △. Side of large △ = 9+18 = 27; 9:6 = 27:?, so ? = 18. A) 12 B) 15 C) 18 D) 21	40. C

The end of the contest ✍ **8**

Solutions

1984-85 Annual 8th Grade Contest
Tuesday, February 12, 1985

8

Contest Information

- **Solutions** Turn the page for detailed contest solutions (written in the question boxes) and letter answers (in the answer columns on the right).

- **Scores** When reviewing these questions, remember *this is a contest, not a test.* There is no "passing" or "failing" score. Few students score as high as 30 points (75% correct); students with even half that, 15 points, *deserve commendation!*

- **Answers & Rating Scale** Turn to page 157 for the letter answers to each question and the rating scale for this contest.

		Answers
1.	If 1985 is divided by 1984, quotient is 1 and remainder is 1. A) $\frac{1}{1984}$ B) $\frac{1984}{1985}$ C) 1 D) $1\frac{1}{1984}$	1. D
2.	Using $\pi = 3.14$, $100\pi = 314$. A) 300 B) 314 C) 315 D) 316	2. B
3.	$1234 + 2143 + 3412 + 4321 = 11\,110$, so choice B is correct. A) 1110 B) 11110 C) 10010 D) 11010	3. B
4.	Since Mickey Mouse can file cards at the rate of 80 cards an hour, after 7 hours he has filed $7 \times 80 = 560$ cards. This leaves $800 - 560 = 240$ cards to be filed. A) 560 B) 140 C) 240 D) 260	4. C
5.	Seventeen thousandths = $17 \times 0.001 = 0.017$. A) 17 000 B) 0.170 C) 0.017 D) 0.0017	5. C
6.	$1000 = 10 \times 100$, so there are 100 tens in 1000. A) 3 B) 10 C) 100 D) 1000	6. C
7.	$\sqrt{144} \times \sqrt{400} = 12 \times 20 = 240$. A) 240 B) 256 C) 576 D) 14 400	7. A
8.	A quadrilateral is a 4-sided polygon; a pentagon has 5 sides. A) square B) trapezoid C) pentagon D) rhombus	8. C
9.	$18 - (-2) = 18 + 2 = 20$; choice A is correct. A) −2 B) −38 C) 2 D) 38	9. A
10.	These numbers are the multiples of 6 between 1 and 100: 6×1, 6×2, 6×3, . . . , 6×15, and 6×16. There are 16 such numbers. A) 6 B) 16 C) 17 D) 96	10. B
11.	$12\frac{1}{2}\% = 12.5\% = 0.125 = 1/8$—none of which equals 12.5 A) 12.5 B) 0.125 C) 12.5% D) $\frac{1}{8}$	11. A
12.	$\frac{3}{2} + \frac{5}{4} + \frac{9}{8} + \frac{17}{16} - 4 = \frac{24}{16} + \frac{20}{16} + \frac{18}{16} + \frac{17}{16} - \frac{64}{16} = \frac{79}{16} - \frac{64}{16} = \frac{15}{16}$. A) $\frac{1}{16}$ B) $\frac{1}{4}$ C) $\frac{1}{2}$ D) $\frac{15}{16}$	12. D
13.	The denominator must be *less* than twice the numerator. A) $\frac{4}{9}$ B) $\frac{5}{11}$ C) $\frac{6}{12}$ D) $\frac{7}{13}$	13. D
14.	$0.0125 = 125/10\,000 = 5/400 = 1/80$. A) $\frac{125}{1000}$ B) $\frac{1}{8}$ C) $\frac{1}{80}$ D) $\frac{12.5}{10\,000}$	14. C
15.	The perimeter of the square is 12, so the length of a side is 3. The area of the square is $3 \times 3 = 9$. A) 9 B) 16 C) 36 D) 81	15. A
16.	$49 \div 0.035 = 49\,000 \div 35 = 1400$. A) 1.4 B) 14 C) 140 D) 1400	16. D

17. The prime numbers between 45 and 65 are 47, 53, 59, and 61. A) 3 B) 4 C) 5 D) 6	17. B
18. Both angles adjacent to the 130° angle are supplementary to it. So $x = 50$, $y = 50$, and $x + y = 100$. A) 50 B) 100 C) 180 D) 260	18. B
19. $\frac{8 \times 9 \times 10}{9 \times 10} \times \frac{6 \times 7}{6 \times 7 \times 8} = 8 \times \frac{9}{9} \times \frac{10}{10} \times \frac{6}{6} \times \frac{7}{7} \times \frac{1}{8} = 8 \times \frac{1}{8} = 1$. A) 1 B) 0 C) $\frac{1}{64}$ D) 65	19. A
20. Since $C = 2\pi r$ (where C is the circumference and r is the radius), the value of $C \div r$ is 2π. A) 1 B) π C) 2 D) 2π	20. D
21. $(-6) - (-7) + (-8) - (9) = (-6) + 7 + (-8) - 9 = 1 - 17 = -16$. A) -30 B) -16 C) 0 D) 2	21. B
22. Area = ½×base×height; so 16 = ½×8×height; or 16 = 4×height. The height must equal 4. A) 1 B) 2 C) 4 D) 8	22. C
23. $\dfrac{4\frac{1}{3}}{4} = \dfrac{4\frac{1}{3} \times 3}{4 \times 3} = \frac{13}{12}$, so the missing number is 13. A) 26 B) 13 C) 8 D) 7	23. B
24. A triangle is a right triangle if the sum of the squares of two sides is equal to the square of the 3rd one; $1^2 + (\sqrt{2})^2 = (\sqrt{3})^2$. A) 9, 16, 25 B) 1, 2, 3 C) 1, $\sqrt{2}$, $\sqrt{3}$ D) 5, 15, 17	24. C
25. $2 \div \frac{1}{2} = 2 \times \frac{2}{1} = 4$, so choice D is correct. A) 1 B) $\frac{1}{4}$ C) 2 D) 4	25. D
26. All 100 integers from 800 to 899 begin with 8. In addition, 708, 718, 728, 738, 748, 758, 768, 778, 788, and 798 end with 8. A) 100 B) 110 C) 120 D) 140	26. B
27. Since $\frac{3}{16} = \frac{1}{4} \times \frac{3}{4}$, $\frac{3}{16}$ of the number is $\frac{1}{4} \times 48 = 12$. A) 12 B) 18 C) 24 D) 192	27. A
28. If the square has sides of length 10, its area is 100. When decreased 10%, length is 9 and area is 81, a decrease if 19%. A) 40% B) 20% C) 19% D) 10%	28. C
29. $1\frac{1}{3} = \frac{4}{3}$; its reciprocal is $\frac{3}{4}$. Now, $\frac{3}{4} - \frac{4}{3} = \frac{9}{12} - \frac{16}{12} = -\frac{7}{12}$. A) $\frac{7}{12}$ B) 0 C) $-\frac{1}{12}$ D) $-\frac{7}{12}$	29. D
30. Coordinates of P and Q are 1.05 and 1.15. Distance from P to Q is 1.15 - 1.05 = 0.10. A) 0.05 B) 0.10 C) 0.50 D) 1.00	30. B

31. Marina types 5 pages in 4 minutes, so she types 75 pages in 1 hour. Ruth types 60 pages in 1 hour, so in 7 hours, Marina types $7 \times 15 = 105$ more pages than Ruth. A) 105 B) 84 C) 15 D) 140	31. A
32. For every 100 people living in the rest of Ontario, 50 people would live in Ontario; and $\frac{50}{150} = \frac{1}{3} = 33\frac{1}{3}\%$ of Ontario's residents would live in Toronto. A) $33\frac{1}{3}\%$ B) 25% C) 20% D) 50%	32. A
33. The 1985th positive odd number is $2 \times 1985 - 1 = 3969$. A) 1985 B) 1987 C) 3969 D) 3971	33. C
34. Since $20\% - 10\% = 10\%$, 10% of the number is 2. If 10% of the number is 2, then 80% of the number equals $8 \times 2 = 16$. A) 4 B) 8 C) 16 D) 32	34. C
35. Since 5 cars plus 8 trucks take up the same room as 11 trucks, 5 cars take up the same room as 3 trucks. Multiply by 10: 50 cars take up the same room as 30 trucks. A) 18 B) 30 C) 50 D) 80	35. C
36. $2^8 \times 5^6 = 2^2 \times 2^6 \times 5^6 = 2^2 \times 10^6 = 4 \times 1\,000\,000 = 4\,000\,000$. A) 4 555 555 B) 2 560 000 C) 4 000 000 D) 5 400 400	36. C
37. There are 33 multiples of 3. Multiples of 3 *and* 4 are multiples of $3 \times 4 = 12$; there are 8 multiples. The fraction is $\frac{8}{33}$. A) $\frac{1}{4}$ B) $\frac{8}{33}$ C) $\frac{25}{33}$ D) $\frac{1}{12}$	37. B
38. $(3*4)*5 = (\frac{7}{12})*5 = \dfrac{\frac{7}{12}+5}{\frac{7}{12} \times 5} = (\frac{7}{12} + \frac{60}{12}) \div \frac{35}{12} = \frac{67}{12} \times \frac{12}{35} = \frac{67}{35}$. A) $\frac{35}{12}$ B) $\frac{67}{420}$ C) $\frac{1}{35}$ D) $\frac{67}{35}$	38. D
39. In choice D, the two squares "topmost" in the drawing would have to overlap; only 5 of a cube's 6 faces would be covered. A) B) C) D)	39. D
40. $\frac{1}{7} = 0.\overline{142857}$, a decimal which repeats in blocks of 6. Every 6th digit is a 7. The 1986th digit is a 7, so the 1985th digit is a 5. A) 2 B) 4 C) 5 D) 8	40. C

The end of the contest   **8**

Solutions

1985-86 Annual 8th Grade Contest

Tuesday, February 11, 1986

8

Contest Information

■ **Solutions** Turn the page for detailed contest solutions (written in the question boxes) and letter answers (in the answer columns on the right).

■ **Scores** When reviewing these questions, remember *this is a contest, not a test*. There is no "passing" or "failing" score. Few students score as high as 30 points (75% correct); students with even half that, 15 points, *deserve commendation!*

■ **Answers & Rating Scale** Turn to page 158 for the letter answers to each question and the rating scale for this contest.

1. $\frac{1}{10} + \frac{2}{10} + \frac{3}{10} + \frac{4}{10} = \frac{10}{10} = 1$.

   A) $\frac{1}{4}$　　　B) $\frac{11}{10}$　　　C) $\frac{7}{30}$　　　D) 1

   1.
   D

2. Carol bought 10 pens at 89¢ per pen, so they cost $8.90. Since $10 − $8.90 = $1.10, choice A is correct.

   A) $1.10　　　B) 79¢　　　C) $9.11　　　D) $2.10

   2.
   A

3. 0.77 + 0.7 = 1.47, so choice B is correct.

   A) 0.84　　　B) 1.47　　　C) 0.777　　　D) 7.77

   3.
   B

4. The measure of each angle of an equilateral triangle is 60°, so the sum of the measures of any two angles is 120°.

   A) 60°　　　B) 90°　　　C) 120°　　　D) 180°

   4.
   C

5. $\frac{21}{56} = \frac{7 \times 3}{7 \times 8} = \frac{7}{7} \times \frac{3}{8} = \frac{3}{8} = 0.375 = 37\frac{1}{2}\%$.

   A) 0.37　　　B) $\frac{3}{4}$　　　C) $37\frac{1}{2}\%$　　　D) $\frac{3}{7}$

   5.
   C

6. 45.2 − 35.3 = (44 − 35) + (1.2 − 0.3) = 9 + 0.9 = 9.9

   A) 9.9　　　B) 10.9　　　C) 10.1　　　D) 9.1

   6.
   A

7. Every 7 days is a Tuesday; 777 = 7×111, so it's a Tuesday.

   A) Monday　　B) Tuesday　　C) Wednesday D) Thursday

   7.
   B

8. $3\frac{5}{6} + \frac{2}{3} = 3\frac{5}{6} + \frac{4}{6} = 3\frac{9}{6} = 4\frac{3}{6} = 4\frac{1}{2}$.

   A) $4\frac{1}{2}$　　　B) $4\frac{1}{3}$　　　C) $4\frac{2}{3}$　　　D) $3\frac{7}{9}$

   8.
   A

9. 0.2 × 0.2 = 0.04, so choice D is correct.

   A) 4　　　B) $\frac{1}{4}$　　　C) 0.4　　　D) 0.04

   9.
   D

10. $\sqrt{25} \times \sqrt{25} = 5\times 5 = 25 = 25\times 1$, so the missing number is 1.

    A) 1　　　B) 5　　　C) 10　　　D) 25

    10.
    A

11. One-fifth of one-fifth $= \frac{1}{5} \times \frac{1}{5} = \frac{1}{25}$.

    A) $\frac{1}{25}$　　　B) $\frac{1}{10}$　　　C) $\frac{1}{5}$　　　D) $\frac{1}{2}$

    11.
    A

12. A right triangle has 1 angle of measure 90° and 2 angles of measure less than 90°. Only choice A is ≤ 90°.

    A) 89°　　　B) 91°　　　C) 93°　　　D) 95°

    12.
    A

13. Since 30:15 = 150:75, the shadow would be 75 m.

    A) 3 m　　　B) 30 m　　　C) 75 m　　　D) 135 m

    13.
    C

14. (−1) × (−2) × (−3) × (−4) = 24; product of 4 negatives is positive.

    A) −24　　　B) −10　　　C) 24　　　D) 10

    14.
    C

15. 49.5÷0.5 = 495÷5 = 99; choice D is most nearly equal to this.

    A) 10　　　B) 25　　　C) 50　　　D) 100

    15.
    D

16. $(1 - \frac{1}{2}) + (\frac{1}{2} - \frac{1}{3}) + (\frac{1}{3} - \frac{1}{4}) = 1 + (\frac{1}{2} - \frac{1}{2}) + (\frac{1}{3} - \frac{1}{3}) - \frac{1}{4} = 1 - \frac{1}{4} = \frac{3}{4}.$ A) 1 B) $1\frac{1}{2}$ C) $\frac{3}{4}$ D) $\frac{1}{4}$	16. C
17. $2^6 - 2^5 = 64 - 32 = 32 = 2^5.$ A) 1 B) 2^1 C) 2^4 D) 2^5	17. D
18. Square I's area is 4; its side is 2 and its perimeter is 8. Square II's perimeter is 24, so its side is 6. The area of square II is 36. A) 12 B) 36 C) 48 D) 144	18. B
19. $\frac{2.4}{5} = \frac{24}{50} = \frac{2 \times 12}{2 \times 25} = \frac{12}{25}$, so choice B is correct. A) $\frac{12}{5}$ B) $\frac{12}{25}$ C) $\frac{6}{125}$ D) $\frac{12}{125}$	19. B
20. The number is $10\frac{1}{2} \div 3 = \frac{21}{2} \times \frac{1}{3} = \frac{7}{2} = 3\frac{1}{2}.$ A) $3\frac{1}{2}$ B) $4\frac{1}{2}$ C) $16\frac{1}{2}$ D) $31\frac{1}{2}$	20. A
21. Since $m\angle a + m\angle b + m\angle c + m\angle d + m\angle e + m\angle f + m\angle g = 360°$ and $m\angle a + m\angle b + m\angle d + m\angle e + m\angle f + m\angle g = 150° + 190° = 340°, m\angle c = 360° - 340° = 20°.$ A) 20° B) 40° C) 50° D) 340°	21. A
22. ½ of a number is 24, so the number is 48; twice the number is 96. A) 12 B) 24 C) 48 D) 96	22. D
23. 0.999 is between 0.9 and 1.0; and it is closer to 1.0. A) 0.1 B) 0.9 C) 0.99 D) 1.0	23. D
24. The sum of two numbers is 11 and their product is 24, so the numbers are 3 and 8. The larger of the two numbers is 8. A) 4 B) 6 C) 8 D) 12	24. C
25. The average of three numbers is 25, so their sum is $3 \times 25 = 75.$ Since $20 + 30 = 50$, the third number is $75 - 50 = 25.$ A) 0 B) 20 C) 25 D) 30	25. C
26. Only choice C, $125\% = 1.25$, is greater than 1. A) 0.125 B) $\frac{3}{24}$ C) 125% D) $\frac{1\frac{1}{2}}{12}$	26. C
27. Choice A differs from 1 by 0.01; no other choice is as close. A) $\frac{99}{100}$ B) $1\frac{1}{99}$ C) 0.9 D) 1.1	27. A
28. If $5 < x < 9$ and $0 < y < 4$, $x > 5$ and $y < 4$, so $x > y$. A) $x < y$ B) $x + y > xy$ C) $xy > 50$ D) $x > y$	28. D
29. $2^7 \times 5^6 = 2 \times 2^6 \times 5^6 = 2 \times (2 \times 5)^6 = 2 \times 10^6 = 2\,000\,000.$ A) 2 555 555 B) 1 280 000 C) 2 000 000 D) 5 200 200	29. C

30. The area of the shaded region is equal to the area of the square minus the area of the circle = $3^2 - \pi \times 1^2$ = $9-\pi$. A) 5 B) $9-\pi$ C) $9-2\pi$ D) $9-4\pi$	30. B
31. Adding (■×■) to ▼ yields ▼, so ■×■ = 0. Thus, ■ = 0. A) −1 B) 0 C) $\frac{1}{2}$ D) 1	31. B
32. If the square has sides of length 10, its area is 100. When increased by 50%, length is 15 and area is 225; increase is 125%. A) 50% B) 100% C) 125% D) 225%	32. C
33. One slice's perimeter = (lengths of 2 radii) + (⅛ of the circumference of whole pizza). Perimeter = $2 \times 8 + \frac{1}{8} \times 16\pi = 16+2\pi$. A) $16 + 2\pi$ B) 2π C) 8π D) $8 + 4\pi$	33. A
34. If the period of 45 consecutive days begins with a Tuesday, there will be a total of 6 Mondays that occur in 45 days. A) 5 B) 6 C) 7 D) 9	34. B
35. Since 5 minutes after class was half over, ⅙ of the period remained, $\frac{1}{2}-\frac{1}{3} = \frac{1}{6}$ = 5 minutes; so $\frac{6}{6}$ = 6×5 = 30 minutes. A) 15 minutes B) 20 minutes C) 24 minutes D) 30 minutes	35. D
36. Each edge is parallel to 3 other edges. There are 12 edges; 12×3 = 36 counts each parallelism twice. The answer is 36÷2 = 18. A) 8 B) 12 C) 16 D) 18	36. D
37. If the difference between two prime numbers is odd, one of them must be even. The primes are 2 and 2 + 1985 = 1987. A) 2431 B) 2002 C) 1987 D) 1986	37. C
38. 2! = 2, 3! = 6, 4! = 24, and 5! = 120. Since 120 is a factor from then on, the units' digit of all the rest is a 0. The units' digit of the sum is the units' digit of 2+6+4+0; this is a 2. A) 0 B) 1 C) 2 D) 3	38. C
39. Since $y = 1985 + x$ and 2000 = $y + x$, 2000 = (1985 + x) + x, and $x = 7\frac{1}{2}$. A) 1990 B) 1995 C) 1999 D) $7\frac{1}{2}$	39. D
40. # of seconds in 2 hrs. = 60×60×2 = 60×24×5 = # of mins. in 5 days. A) 1 day B) 2 days C) 4 days D) 5 days	40. D

The end of the contest ☞ **8**

Solutions

1986-87 Annual 8th Grade Contest

Tuesday, February 10, 1987

8

Contest Information

- **Solutions** Turn the page for detailed contest solutions (written in the question boxes) and letter answers (in the answer columns on the right).

- **Scores** When reviewing these questions, remember *this is a contest, not a test.* There is no "passing" or "failing" score. Few students score as high as 30 points (75% correct); students with even half that, 15 points, *deserve commendation!*

- **Answers & Rating Scale** Turn to page 159 for the letter answers to each question and the rating scale for this contest.

1. 198^7 is the product of 7 even numbers, so it must be even. A) 198^7 B) $19{\times}87$ C) 19^{87} D) $1{+}9{+}87$	1. A
2. 100% of 50 = 1 × 50 = 50. A) 5000 B) 500 C) 50 D) 0.5	2. C
3. $0.04 = \frac{4}{100} = \frac{2}{50} \neq \frac{2}{5}$, so choice D is correct. A) $\frac{4}{10}$ B) $\frac{22}{55}$ C) 40% D) 0.04	3. D
4. If the product of two whole numbers is 100, the numbers could be 100 and 1. Since 100 + 1 = 101, choice A is correct. A) 101 B) 52 C) 29 D) 20	4. A
5. $\frac{5}{6} \times \frac{6}{7} \times \frac{7}{8} \times \frac{8}{9} = \frac{5}{1} \times \frac{6}{6} \times \frac{7}{7} \times \frac{8}{8} \times \frac{1}{9} = \frac{5}{1} \times \frac{1}{9} = \frac{5}{9}$. A) $\frac{1}{9}$ B) 1 C) $\frac{9}{5}$ D) $\frac{5}{9}$	5. D
6. $\sqrt{25^2} = (\sqrt{25})^2 = 5^2 = 25$. A) 5 B) 25 C) 312.5 D) 625	6. B
7. 19 m + 87 cm = 1900 cm + 87 cm = 1987 cm. A) 0.1987 cm B) 19.87 cm C) 198.7 cm D) 1987 cm	7. D
8. $\frac{\pi}{2} - \frac{\pi}{3} = \frac{3\pi}{6} - \frac{2\pi}{6} = \frac{3\pi - 2\pi}{6} = \frac{\pi}{6}$. A) $\frac{1}{6}$ B) $\frac{\pi}{6}$ C) $\frac{2\pi}{6}$ D) $\frac{5\pi}{6}$	8. B
9. Numerator of Choice A is more than one-half its denominator. A) $\frac{100}{199}$ B) $\frac{1}{2}$ C) $\frac{49}{99}$ D) $\frac{98}{197}$	9. A
10. $\frac{0.77}{2} = 0.77 \div 2 = 0.385$, so choice A is correct. A) 0.385 B) 1.54 C) 3.85 D) 38.5	10. A
11. Both 1986 and 1988 are divisible by 2; 1985 is divisible by 5. A) 1985 B) 1986 C) 1987 D) 1988	11. C
12. If the bell rings every 2 seconds and the bird chirps every 3 seconds, the ring and chirp occur together every 6 seconds. So they occur together again in multiples of 6 seconds; 42 = 7×6. A) 40 seconds B) 41 seconds C) 42 seconds D) 43 seconds	12. C
13. (5% of 40) + (15% of 40) = (20% of 40) = (10% of 80). A) 5% B) 10% C) 20% D) 40%	13. B
14. $m\angle ABD = \frac{1}{2} \times m\angle ABC = \frac{1}{2} \times 90° = 45°$. A) 180° B) 90° C) 50° D) 45°	14. D
15. If $B = 100$, then $A = 125$; so B is 20% less than A. A) 10% B) 15% C) 20% D) 25%	15. C

Go on to the next page ▨▨▨➡ **8**

16.	$3\times4\times5 = 60 = 20 + 40 = (4\times5) + (8\times5)$; choice D is correct. A) 3 B) 3×5 C) 8 D) 8×5	16. D
17.	$\frac{1}{4} \times \frac{1}{4} \times \frac{1}{4} = \frac{1}{64} = \frac{16}{64 \times 16} = 16 \times \frac{1}{1024} = 4 \times 4 \times \frac{1}{1024}.$ A) $\frac{1}{1024}$ B) $\frac{1}{64}$ C) $\frac{1}{4}$ D) 4	17. A
18.	10 seconds:10 hours = 1 second:1 hour = $1:(60\times60)$ = 1:3600. A) $\frac{1}{60}$ B) $\frac{1}{360}$ C) $\frac{1}{3600}$ D) $\frac{1}{36000}$	18. C
19.	$0.48\div0.016 = 480\div16 = 30$, so choice B is correct. A) 300 B) 30 C) 3 D) 0.3	19. B
20.	$0.05 = 0.050$; $\frac{1}{5} = .200$; $\frac{1}{2}\% = 0.5\% = 0.005$; $0.1 = 0.100$. A) 0.05 B) $\frac{1}{5}$ C) $\frac{1}{2}\%$ D) 0.1	20. C
21.	$4000\div7 = 571\frac{3}{7}$; so it takes 572 sevens to first exceed 4000. A) 4001 B) 572 C) 571 D) 470	21. B
22.	$\frac{1}{2}:2\frac{1}{2} = (2\times\frac{1}{2}):(2\times2\frac{1}{2}) = 1:5$, so choice C is correct. A) $\frac{1}{2}$ B) $\frac{1}{4}$ C) $\frac{1}{5}$ D) $\frac{1}{8}$	22. C
23.	If the average of 3 numbers is between 7 and 10, the sum of the numbers is between $3\times7 = 21$ and $3\times10 = 30$. A) 20 B) 22 C) 26 D) 28	23. A
24.	If ¾ of a number is 24, ¼ of it is 8 and the number is 32. A) 32 B) 30 C) 18 D) 16	24. A
25.	If 2 cm represents 50 meters, then $(2\div10)$ cm represents $(50\div10)$ meters; so 0.2 cm represents 5 meters. A) 10 B) 0.02 C) 0.2 D) $\frac{1}{10}$	25. C
26.	Undo the process: $25\div3 = 8\frac{1}{3}$; $8\frac{1}{3} - 2 = 6\frac{1}{3}$; choice D is closest. A) 11 B) 10 C) 7 D) 6	26. D
27.	$6^2 + 8^2 - 10^2 = 36 + 64 - 100 = 0$, so choice A is correct. A) 0 B) 4 C) 6 D) 12	27. A
28.	If a whole number is first multiplied by 2 and then by 5. The result must be a multiple of $2\times5 = 10$, so choice C is correct. A) 12 B) 25 C) 50 D) 55	28. C
29.	Using $\pi = 3.14$, $99\pi = 100\pi - 1\pi = 314 - 3.14 = 310.86$ A) 310 B) 311 C) 313 D) 314	29. B

Go on to the next page ⏩ **8**

30. It takes $1500 \div 10 = 150$ cartons with 10 books per carton; it takes $1500 \div 15 = 100$ cartons with 15 books per carton. A) 5 B) 50 C) 100 D) 500	30. B
31. The square of $\frac{1}{4}$ is $\frac{1}{16}$ and the square root of $\frac{1}{256}$ is $\frac{1}{16}$. A) $\frac{1}{2}$ B) $\frac{1}{4}$ C) $\frac{1}{16}$ D) $\frac{1}{256}$	31. D
32. The perimeter of the equilateral triangle is $\frac{1}{2} \times 24 = 12$. Since all 3 sides are equal, the length of a side is $12 \div 3 = 4$. A) 4 B) 6 C) 8 D) 12	32. A
33. Al is four times as old as Carl. Since in 10 years, Al will be twice as old as Carl, Al is 20 and Carl is 5. A) 40 B) 20 C) 10 D) 5	33. B
34. As shown in the diagram, $AB = BC = CD$, so AC is 200% of CD. 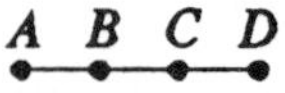 A B C D A) 25% B) 50% C) 100% D) 200%	34. D
35. b books:d dollars = 1 book:$\frac{d}{b}$ dollars = d books:$\frac{d^2}{b}$ dollars. A) b dollars B) bd dollars C) $\frac{d^2}{b}$ dollars D) $\frac{b^2}{d}$ dollars	35. C
36. Each revolution the wheel moves $\pi \times 2$ meters. Using $\pi = 3.14$, it moves 6.28 m/revolution; $100 \div 6.28$ is closest to choice C. A) 64 B) 32 C) 16 D) 8	36. C
37. The volume of cube I is $10^3 = 1000$. The volume of cube II is $1000 + 331 = 1331$. Since $11^3 = 1331$, cube II's edge is 11. A) 14 meters B) 13 meters C) 12 meters D) 11 meters	37. D
38. Action Comic #1 has increased in value 1 849 990¢. The percent increase is $\frac{1849990}{10} \times 100\% = 18\,499\,900\%$. A) 18 500 000% B) 185 000% C) 1 849 990% D) 18 499 900%	38. D
39. Travelling in the same direction, the distance between them is 200 km ± 15 km. Travelling in opposite directions, the distance is 200 km ± 115 km, so the *unattainable* distance is 115 km. A) 85 km B) 115 km C) 185 km D) 215 km	39. B
40. The 1st few terms are 12, 6, 3, 10, 5, 16, 8, 4, 2, 1, 4, 2, 1, ..., and the 4, 2, 1 continues. From the 10th term on, every 3rd term is 1. Hence, 990 terms later, the 1000th term will be a 1. Choice A is correct. A) 1 B) 2 C) 3 D) 4	40. A

The end of the contest ✍ **8**

Solutions

1987-88 Annual 8th Grade Contest
Tuesday, February 2, 1988

8

Contest Information

- **Solutions** Turn the page for detailed contest solutions (written in the question boxes) and letter answers (in the answer columns on the right).

- **Scores** When reviewing these questions, remember *this is a contest, not a test.* There is no "passing" or "failing" score. Few students score as high as 30 points (75% correct); students with even half that, 15 points, *deserve commendation!*

- **Answers & Rating Scale** Turn to page 160 for the letter answers to each question and the rating scale for this contest.

1.	$7\times25¢ + 6\times10¢ + 5\times5¢ + 4\times1¢ = \$1.75 + \$0.60 + \$0.25 + \$0.04 = \$2.64.$ A) 22¢ B) \$1.64 C) \$2.64 D) \$3.64	1. C
2.	$1988 - \frac{1985}{1988} = 1987\frac{1988}{1988} - \frac{1985}{1988} = 1987\frac{1988-1985}{1988} = 1987\frac{3}{1988}.$ A) $1987\frac{3}{1988}$ B) $1987\frac{1985}{1988}$ C) $1988\frac{3}{1988}$ D) $1988\frac{1985}{1988}$	2. A
3.	$(10-9) + (8-7) + (6-5) + (4-3) + (2-1) = 5.$ A) 9 B) 5 C) 3 D) 1	3. B
4.	If the product of two whole numbers is 100 and one of the numbers is 48 more than the other, the numbers are 2 and 50. A) 2 B) 48 C) 50 D) 96	4. C
5.	$\frac{19}{88} \times \frac{88}{19} = \frac{19\times88}{88\times19} = \frac{19}{19} \times \frac{88}{88} = 1 \times 1 = 1.$ A) 1 B) $\frac{1988}{8819}$ C) $\frac{19}{88}$ D) 0	5. A
6.	Since $AC = BC$, $\angle A = \angle B$. $\angle A + \angle B = 180° - \angle C = 180° - 60° = 120°$. So $\angle B = 120°÷2 = 60°$. A) 60° B) 45° C) 30° D) 12°	6. A
7.	$\sqrt{16\times16} = \sqrt{16} \times \sqrt{16} = 4 \times 4 = 16.$ A) 2 B) 4 C) 8 D) 16	7. D
8.	Use a number line to see that $-\frac{7}{3} = -2\frac{1}{3} > -2\frac{1}{2} = -\frac{5}{2}.$ A) $-\frac{8}{3}$ B) $-\frac{7}{3}$ C) $-\frac{7}{2}$ D) -3	8. B
9.	If I walk around this lot once, I walk a distance equal to the perimeter of the lot; perimeter $= 2\times(42\text{ m} + 26\text{ m}) = 136$ m. A) 68 m B) 104 m C) 136 m D) 272 m	9. C
10.	$\frac{2}{3}÷\frac{3}{2} = \frac{2}{3} \times \frac{2}{3} = \frac{2\times2}{3\times3} = \frac{4}{9}.$ A) 1 B) $\frac{4}{9}$ C) $\frac{9}{4}$ D) 0	10. B
11.	$0.19 + 0.88 = 1.07$, so choice D is correct. A) 0.1988 B) 0.278 C) 0.97 D) 1.07	11. D
12.	Since 50% of \$200 = \$100 and \$200 + \$100 = \$300, choice B is correct. A) \$150 B) \$200 C) \$250 D) \$275	12. B
13.	A side of the larger square is 5 and a side of the smaller square is 4. Their areas are 25 and 16; the area of the region between the two squares is $25 - 16 = 9.$ A) 1 B) 2 C) 4 D) 9	13. D
14.	$0.66 = \frac{66}{100} = \frac{2\times33}{2\times50} = \frac{33}{50}$, so choice D is correct. A) $\frac{1}{3}$ B) $\frac{2}{3}$ C) $\frac{6}{7}$ D) $\frac{33}{50}$	14. D

Go on to the next page ⟹ **8**

15. $\frac{20\%}{100} = 0.20 \div 100 = \frac{20}{100} \times \frac{1}{100} = \frac{1}{5} \times \frac{1}{100} = \frac{1}{5 \times 100} = \frac{1}{500}.$ A) $\frac{1}{5}$ B) $\frac{1}{50}$ C) $\frac{1}{500}$ D) $\frac{1}{5000}$	15. C
16. They need $100 \times 2 = 200$ slices. Since each pizza has 8 slices, they ordered $200 \div 8 = 25$ pizzas. A) 50 pizzas B) 25 pizzas C) 200 pizzas D) 100 pizzas	16. B
17. $(-1)^{1989} - (-1)^{1988} = -1 - 1 = -2.$ A) -2 B) -1 C) 0 D) 2	17. A
18. If 2 cm represents 50 km., 1 cm represents 25 km. So their actual distance apart is $7.5 \times 25 = 187.5$ km. A) 375 km B) 275 km C) 187.5 km D) 75 km	18. C
19. $(\frac{1}{3} \times 11) + (\frac{1}{3} \times 13) = \frac{1}{3} \times (11 + 13) = \frac{1}{3} \times 24.$ A) $\frac{1}{3} \times 12$ B) $\frac{1}{3} \times 24$ C) $\frac{2}{3} \times 12$ D) $\frac{2}{3} \times 24$	19. B
20. A cube has 8 vertices, so choice C is correct. A) 4 B) 6 C) 8 D) 12	20. C
21. $\angle 1 + \angle 2 + \angle ABC = 180°$. Since $\triangle ABC$ is an equilateral triangle, $\angle ABC = 60°$. So $\angle 1 + \angle 2 + 60° = 180°$, $\angle 1 + \angle 2 = 120°$. A) $60°$ B) $90°$ C) $120°$ D) $180°$	21. C
22. Choice A is less than 1 and its reciprocal is greater than 1. A) $\frac{1987}{1988}$ B) $\frac{1988}{1987}$ C) $1\frac{1}{3}$ D) $-\frac{2}{3}$	22. A
23. The number of eighths in $5.75 = 5.75 \div \frac{1}{8} = 5.75 \times 8 = 46.$ A) 8 B) 23 C) 46 D) 120	23. C
24. Steve's jogging time increased by $\frac{1}{2}$ hour. Since $\frac{1}{2}:2\frac{1}{2} = 1:5$, this is a 20% increase. A) 10% B) 20% C) 25% D) 50%	24. B
25. Undo each operation: $\frac{3}{8} \times 6 = \frac{18}{8}; \frac{18}{8} \div 5 = \frac{18}{40} = \frac{9}{20}.$ A) $\frac{5}{16}$ B) $\frac{5}{6}$ C) $\frac{6}{5}$ D) $\frac{9}{20}$	25. D
26. $75\% - \frac{2}{3} = \frac{75}{100} - \frac{2}{3} = \frac{3}{4} - \frac{2}{3} = \frac{9}{12} - \frac{8}{12} = \frac{1}{12}.$ A) $\frac{1}{12}$ B) $\frac{1}{10}$ C) $\frac{1}{9}$ D) $\frac{3}{10}$	26. A
27. If the square root of the area of a square is 25, the area of the square is $25^2 = 625$. A) 625 B) 100 C) 25 D) 5	27. A
28. Since $C = 2\pi r$, then $C \div r = 2\pi$. A) $\frac{\pi}{2}$ B) π C) $\frac{3\pi}{2}$ D) 2π	28. D

29. Since $\frac{1}{2} \times \frac{1}{2} = \frac{1}{4}$, the square root of $\frac{1}{4}$ is $\frac{1}{2}$. A) $\frac{1}{2}$　　　B) $\frac{1}{8}$　　　C) $\frac{1}{16}$　　　D) $\frac{1}{64}$	29. A
30. $2.5:7.5 = (2\times2.5):(2\times7.5) = 5:15 = 1:3$. A) 2:7　　　B) 7:2　　　C) 3:1　　　D) 1:3	30. D
31. ¼ of 520 cm is 130 cm, so 520 cm – 130 cm = 390 cm remains after first cut. $\frac{4}{5}$ of 390 cm = 312 cm, leaving 78 cm of the log. A) 26 cm　　B) 78 cm　　C) 104 cm　　D) 312 cm	31. B
32. Since $OA = OB$, $m\angle A = m\angle B$. Also, $m\angle O = m\angle A$. So all three angles in $\triangle OAB$ have equal measures, and the measure of angle B is $180° \div 3 = 60°$. A) 30°　　　B) 45°　　　C) 60°　　　D) 180°	32. C
33. One of the years must be a leap year, so #1988 + #1989 + #1990 + #1991 = 366 + 365 + 365 + 365 = 1461. A) 1460　　B) 1461　　C) 1462　　D) 1463	33. B
34. The sum of two odd numbers is always an even number, so the sum could not odd; and 161 is odd. A) 161　　　B) 168　　　C) 186　　　D) 196	34. A
35. $900^2 < 999^2 < 1000^2$ or $810\,000 < 999^2 < 1\,000\,000$; so $10^5 < 999^2 < 10^6$. A) 10^3 and 10^4　B) 10^4 and 10^5　C) 10^5 and 10^6　D) 10^6 and 10^7	35. C
36. $x + 3$ is an even number, so x is an odd number. Then $x + 1$ and $3x + 5$ are even; but, since $5x$ is odd, $5x + 8$ is also odd. A) $x + 1$　　B) $6x + 4$　　C) $3x + 5$　　D) $5x + 8$	36. D
37. The sum of the first 1 million primes consists of 1 even number, 2, and 999 999 odd numbers. This sum is odd. A) 1　　　B) 2　　　C) 3　　　D) 9	37. B
38. Since $\frac{6a}{5b} = \frac{6}{5} \times \frac{a}{b}$ and $\frac{a}{b} = 5\%$, then $\frac{6a}{5b} = \frac{6}{5} \times 5\% = \frac{6}{5} \times \frac{5}{100} = \frac{6}{100}$. A) 6%　　B) 25%　　C) 30%　　D) $\frac{6}{5}\%$	38. A
39. The minute hand moves 12 times as fast as the hour hand. Therefore, if the minute hand moves 180°, the hour hand must move $180° \div 12 = 15°$. A) 2.5°　　B) 15°　　C) 20°　　D) 30°	39. B
40. Together, Jack and Jill bought 5 hamburgers and 5 shakes and spent $9.45. One-fifth of that is the cost of 1 hamburger and 1 shake. Since $9.45÷5 = $1.89, choice C is correct. A) $1.03　　B) $1.54　　C) $1.89　　D) $9.45	40. C

The end of the contest 🖎 **8**

Solutions

1988-89 Annual 8th Grade Contest
Tuesday, February 7, 1989

8

Contest Information

■ **Solutions** Turn the page for detailed contest solutions (written in the question boxes) and letter answers (in the answer columns on the right).

■ **Scores** When reviewing these questions, remember *this is a contest, not a test*. There is no "passing" or "failing" score. Few students score as high as 30 points (75% correct); students with even half that, 15 points, *deserve commendation!*

■ **Answers & Rating Scale** Turn to page 161 for the letter answers to each question and the rating scale for this contest.

1. $19.90 - 19.89 = 0.90 - 0.89 = 0.01.$ A) 1 B) 0.1 C) 0.01 D) 0.001	1. C
2. When the price of the *Times-Herald* was increased from 25¢ to 30¢, this represented a price increase of 5¢; 5:25 = 1:5 = 20%. A) 5% B) $16\frac{2}{3}$% C) 20% D) 25%	2. C
3. $\frac{1}{9} + \frac{2}{9} + \frac{3}{9} + \frac{4}{9} + \frac{5}{9} + \frac{6}{9} + \frac{7}{9} + \frac{8}{9} = \frac{36}{9} = 4.$ A) 1 B) 4 C) 8 D) 16	3. B
4. The value of 10 nickels = the value of 5 dimes; the value of 20 nickels and 10 dimes = the value of 10 nickels and 15 dimes. A) 5 B) 15 C) 20 D) 25	4. B
5. $(10 \times 0.01) + (100 \times 0.002) + (1000 \times 0.0003) = 0.1 + 0.2 + 0.3 = 0.6.$ A) 0.0123 B) 0.6 C) 0.06 D) 0.006	5. B
6. The area of the rectangle is $10 \times 20 = 200$. Since one-fourth is shaded, the area of the shaded region is $200 \div 4 = 50$. A) 200 B) 100 C) 50 D) 40	6. C
7. $\frac{1}{2} + \frac{1}{3} + \frac{1}{6} = \frac{3}{6} + \frac{2}{6} + \frac{1}{6} = \frac{6}{6} = 1.$ A) 1 B) 11 C) $\frac{1}{11}$ D) 36	7. A
8. $\sqrt{1+4+1+4+1+4+1+4+1+4} = \sqrt{25} = 5.$ A) 5 B) 15 C) 25 D) 225	8. A
9. $\frac{1}{3} \times \frac{1}{3} = \frac{1}{9} = \frac{1}{2} \times \frac{2}{9}$, so choice D is correct. A) $\frac{1}{2}$ B) $\frac{1}{9}$ C) $\frac{1}{18}$ D) $\frac{2}{9}$	9. D
10. The sum of two consecutive integers is *always* an odd number. A) –1 B) 0 C) 1 D) 1989	10. B
11. $35\% + 40\% = 0.35 + 0.40 = 0.75 = ¾.$ A) $\frac{3}{5}$ B) $\frac{3}{4}$ C) $\frac{4}{5}$ D) $\frac{5}{6}$	11. B
12. $(1 + 2 + 3 + 4 + 5)^2 - (1^2 + 2^2 + 3^2 + 4^2 + 5^2) = 15^2 - (1 + 4 + 9 + 16 + 25) = 225 - 55 = 170.$ A) 0 B) 15 C) 55 D) 170	12. D
13. $(2 \times 3 \times 4) \times (\frac{1}{2} + \frac{1}{3} + \frac{1}{4}) = 24 \times (\frac{6}{12} + \frac{4}{12} + \frac{3}{12}) = 24 \times \frac{13}{12} = 2 \times 13 = 26.$ A) 1 B) 3 C) 24 D) 26	13. D
14. Choices are, in order, –0.100, –0.010, –0.110, & –0.011. C is least. A) $-\frac{1}{10}$ B) $-\frac{1}{100}$ C) $-\frac{11}{100}$ D) $-\frac{11}{1000}$	14. C
15. There is one 90° angle and two 45° angles. A) 45° B) 60° C) 90° D) 180°	15. A

16.	The average number of home runs Roger Maris hit per game was $61 \div 162 \approx 0.38$ A) 0.03 B) 0.38 C) 2.66 D) 32.15	16. B
17.	$(2\times22\times40) - (2\times22\times 39) = (2\times22)\times(40 - 39) = 2\times22\times1 = 44.$ A) 22 B) 39 C) 40 D) 44	17. D
18.	$\frac{98}{76 \times 54} = \frac{98\div100}{(76\times54)\div100} = \frac{98\div100}{(76\div10)\times(54\div10)} = \frac{0.98}{7.6 \times 5.4}.$ A) $\frac{0.98}{7.6 \times 5.4}$ B) $\frac{0.98}{0.76 \times 0.54}$ C) $\frac{9.8}{0.76 \times 54}$ D) $\frac{9.8}{0.76 \times 5.4}$	18. A
19.	5 hours before 1 P.M. is 8 A.M.; 15 minutes later is 8:15 A.M. A) 5:45 A.M. B) 8:15 A.M. C) 8:45 A.M. D) 9:15 A.M.	19. B
20.	100% of 100% $= 1.00\times1.00 = 1.$ A) 1 B) 2 C) 200 D) 10000	20. A
21.	If p is a prime number, then $p + 2$ is sometimes a prime number. For example, both 3 and $3 + 2$ are prime numbers. A) $p + 7$ B) $p + 2$ C) $p + p$ D) $p\times p$	21. B
22.	$\frac{2}{3} \div 0.33333 = 0.66666\frac{2}{3} \div 0.33333 \approx 0.66666 \div 0.33333 = 2.$ A) $\frac{2}{9}$ B) $\frac{1}{9}$ C) 1 D) 2	22. D
23.	$1989 - 1989\frac{1}{2} = -(1989\frac{1}{2} - 1989) = -\frac{1}{2}.$ A) $\frac{1}{2}$ B) 0 C) $-\frac{1}{2}$ D) $-1\frac{1}{2}$	23. C
24.	$\frac{10^8 - 1}{101} = \frac{100\,000\,000 - 1}{101} = \frac{99\,999\,999}{101} = 990\,099.$ A) 9999 B) 90909 C) 990099 D) 909090	24. C
25.	Since 1 CD costs twice as much as 1 cassette, 7 cassettes also cost \$42. Thus, 1 cassette costs \$6 and 1 CD costs \$12. A) \$12 B) \$15 C) \$16 D) \$18	25. D
26.	One-half of 1% $= 0.5\% = 0.005.$ A) 0.5 B) 0.05 C) 0.005 D) 0.0005	26. C
27.	If a *left angle* were defined as the supplement of a right angle, then the measure of a *left angle* would be $180°-90° = 90°.$ A) 0° B) 45° C) 90° D) 180°	27. C
28.	2 m $- 2$ cm $= 2.00$ m $- 0.02$ m $= 1.98$ m. A) 1.98 m B) 198 m C) 1.8 m D) 18 m	28. A
29.	If Mom takes 5 minutes to do each thing, she will be done in 5 million minutes; since $5\,000\,000 \div 60 = 83\,333\frac{1}{3}$, D is correct. A) 120000 B) 200000 C) $66\,666\frac{2}{3}$ D) $83\,333\frac{1}{3}$	29. D

30. $\frac{1.21}{1.1} = \frac{1.1 \times 1.1}{1.1} = \frac{1.1}{1}$, so choice A is correct. A) 1 B) 1.1 C) 10 D) 11		30. A
31. The side of the larger square is 14 and the side of the smaller square is 10. The area between the squares is $14^2 - 10^2 = 96$ and the area of the shaded region is $96 \div 4 = 24$. A) 4 B) 16 C) 20 D) 24		31. D
32. Undo each operation: $1 - 2 = -1$; $-1 \div 100 = -0.01$. A) −1.00 B) −0.01 C) 0.01 D) 0.03		32. B
33. Since $5 \times 0 = 0$, $x = 0$. A) 0 B) 1 C) $\frac{1}{5}$ D) 5		33. A
34. $\frac{\pi}{2} > \frac{\pi}{3} > 1 > \frac{\pi}{4} > \frac{\pi}{5}$; so B is larger than A. Since $\frac{\pi}{4} < 1$ and $\frac{\pi}{5} < 1$, both C and D are less than B. A) $\frac{\pi}{2}$ B) $\frac{\pi}{2} \times \frac{\pi}{3}$ C) $\frac{\pi}{2} \times \frac{\pi}{3} \times \frac{\pi}{4}$ D) $\frac{\pi}{3} \times \frac{\pi}{4} \times \frac{\pi}{5}$		34. B
35. $10 = 2^1 + 2^3$, so $a + b = 1 + 3 = 4$. A) 3 B) 4 C) 5 D) 6		35. B
36. On each revolution, a point 2 m from the center travels twice as far as a point 1 m from the center. So the point 2 m from the center travels twice as fast as the point 1 m from the center. A) 900 m/sec B) 1800 m/sec C) 2700 m/sec D) 3600 m/sec		36. B
37. To maximize the difference, the ones' digit of the rounded-off number would have to be a 5. The difference can never be 6. A) 3 B) 4 C) 5 D) 6		37. D
38. Tripling each side multiplies the area by $3 \times 3 = 9$, so the answer is $9 \times 15 = 45$. A) 8 B) 15 C) 45 D) 225		38. C
39. The smallest parallelogram P is the 2 by 3 shaded rectangle shown in the diagram. The area of this parallelogram P is 6. A) 2 B) 4 C) 6 D) 14		39. C
40. Add 1 to each of the 1st 100 positive odd numbers to form the 1st 100 positive even numbers; so the sum is $100^2 + 100$. A) 100^2 B) $100^2 + 1$ C) $100^2 + 50$ D) $100^2 + 100$		40. D

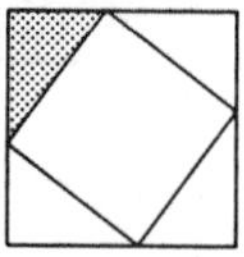

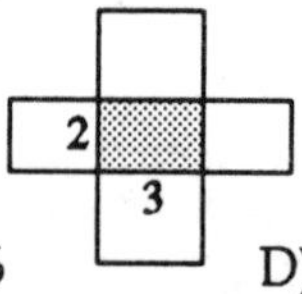

The end of the contest ✍ **8**

1989-90 Annual 8th Grade Contest

Tuesday, February 6, 1990

8

Contest Information

■ **Solutions** Turn the page for detailed contest solutions (written in the question boxes) and letter answers (in the answer columns on the right).

■ **Scores** When reviewing these questions, remember *this is a contest, not a test*. There is no "passing" or "failing" score. Few students score as high as 30 points (75% correct); students with even half that, 15 points, *deserve commendation!*

■ **Answers & Rating Scale** Turn to page 162 for the letter answers to each question and the rating scale for this contest.

1.	$\frac{1000}{1990} + \frac{900}{1990} + \frac{90}{1990} = \frac{1000 + 900 + 90}{1990} = \frac{1990}{1990} = 1.$	1.
	A) 0 B) 1 C) 1990 D) $\frac{1}{1990}$	B
2.	I arrived at Pat's house at 9:10 A.M. If I left Pat's house 360 minutes later, I left Pat's house 6 hours later or 3:10 P.M.	2.
	A) 9:46 A.M. B) 9:10 P.M. C) 3:10 A.M. D) 3:10 P.M.	D
3.	0.222 + 0.333 + 0.444 = 0.999, so choice B is correct.	3.
	A) 1 B) 0.999 C) 0.99 D) 0.9	B
4.	1990 = 1×2×5×199; 9 is *not* a factor.	4.
	A) 1 B) 2 C) 5 D) 9	D
5.	$\frac{1}{3} + \frac{1}{6} = \frac{2}{6} + \frac{1}{6} = \frac{3}{6} = \frac{1}{2} = \frac{2}{4} = \frac{1}{4} + \frac{1}{4}$, so choice C is correct.	5.
	A) $\frac{1}{8}$ B) $\frac{1}{7}$ C) $\frac{1}{4}$ D) $\frac{1}{2}$	C
6.	(0.21÷0.07)÷0.03 = (21÷7)÷0.03 = 3÷0.03 = 300÷3 = 100.	6.
	A) 0.01 B) 1 C) 10 D) 100	D
7.	999+998+997+996 = 1000×4 - (1+2+3+4) = 4000 - 10.	7.
	A) 4 B) 7 C) 10 D) 15	C
8.	The total number of students in Mr. Room's five classes is 18 + 19 + 20 + 21 + 22 = 5×20 = 100.	8.
	A) 5 B) 20 C) 100 D) 110	C
9.	2 × 4 + 6 ÷ 2 = (2×4) + (6÷2) = 8 + 3 = 11.	9.
	A) 14 B) 11 C) 10 D) 110	B
10.	The largest whole number less than 200 is 199; the smallest whole number greater than 200 is 201. Their sum is 400.	10.
	A) 200 B) 201 C) 300 D) 400	D
11.	22×24×26 = 11×2×12×2×13×2 = 11×12×13×8.	11.
	A) 16 B) 8 C) 6 D) 2	B
12.	100% × 100% = 1.00×1.00 = 1.00 = 100%.	12.
	A) 100% B) 200% C) 1000% D) 10000%	A
13.	The six positive whole number factors of 12 are 1, 2, 3, 4, 6, and 12. The product of these factors is 1×2×3×4×6×12 = 1728.	13.
	A) 12 B) 72 C) 144 D) 1728	D
14.	Since the last factor is 0, the product is equal to 0.	14.
	A) 0 B) –15 C) 120 D) –120	A
15.	(41 + 43)÷2 = 42.	15.
	A) 40 B) 41 C) 42 D) 43	C

Go on to the next page ⟹ **8**

16. $\frac{1}{3} : \frac{1}{9} = \frac{1}{3} \div \frac{1}{9} = \frac{1}{3} \times \frac{9}{1} = \frac{3}{1} = 3:1.$

   A) 3:1   B) 3:9   C) 1:3   D) $1:\frac{1}{27}$

16.

A

17. 62.5% of the pizza $= \frac{625}{1000}$ of the pizza $= \frac{5}{8} \times 8$ slices $= 5$ slices.

   A) 3 slices   B) 5 slices   C) 1/8 slice   D) 5/8 slice

17.

B

18. $10.01 \times 10 \times 9.99$ is approximately equal to $10 \times 10 \times 10 = 10^3$.

   A) 10   B) 10^2 C) 10^3 D) 10^4

18.

C

19. If the string is cut into 38 equal pieces, 19 of these pieces is one-half of the string or 50 m.

   A) (100/38) m   B) 38 m   C) 19 m   D) 50 m

19.

D

20. $3 \times 4 = (1.5 \times 2) \times 4 = 1.5 \times (2 \times 4) = 1.5 \times 8.$

   A) 2   B) 2.5   C) 8   D) 8.5

20.

C

21. The reciprocal of 0.5 is 2; the others have smaller reciprocals.

   A) 0.5   B) 1   C) 1989   D) 1990

21.

A

22. $C = 2\pi r = 12\pi$, so $r = 6$. $A = \pi r^2 = \pi \times 6^2 = 36\pi.$

   A) 144π B) 36π C) 9π D) 6π

22.

B

23. A two-digit whole number is added to a three-digit whole number. The *least* possible value of this sum is $10 + 100 = 110$.

   A) 199   B) 110   C) 109   D) 101

23.

B

24. $\sqrt{(-9) \times (-9)} = \sqrt{81} = 9$; the other choices are all less than 9.

   A) $\frac{80}{9}$ B) $\sqrt{80}$ C) $\frac{89}{10}$ D) $\sqrt{(-9) \times (-9)}$

24.

D

25. 4 m:3 kg $= (4 \times 4\text{m}):(4 \times 3 \text{ kg}) = 16$ m:12 kg, so the second piece has a length of 16 m.

   A) 48 m   B) 16 m   C) 9 m   D) 1 m

25.

B

26. Since $AB = AD$, $m\angle ADB = m\angle ABD$. Since $m\angle A = 60°$, $m\angle ADB + m\angle ABD = 120°$; each is 60°. So $\triangle ABD$ is equilateral and its perimeter is $3 \times 12 = 36$.

   A) 12   B) 24   C) 36   D) 144

26.

C

27. Since 51 is *composite* ($51 = 3 \times 17$), no prime is divisible by it.

   A) 0   B) 1   C) 3   D) 51

27.

A

28. The average of 7 numbers is 7, so their sum is 49. The largest is at most $49 - (1 + 2 + 3 + 4 + 5 + 6) = 28$.

   A) 49   B) 43   C) 28   D) 20

28.

C

29. Since $1000 = 125 \times 8$, every such number is divisible by 125.

   A) 80   B) 125   C) 400   D) 625

29.

B

Go on to the next page ⟫ **8**

30. GCF is 1 – both numbers are the products of different primes. A) 1 B) 2 C) 6 D) 10	30. A
31. Of the 24 radii, only 22 (not the 2 end ones) connect the given centers. Since 22 radii = 11 diameters, the distance = 11×1 cm = 11 cm. A) 10 cm B) 11 cm C) 12 cm D) 13 cm	31. B
32. $\sqrt{\dfrac{3^2 + 4^2}{5^2}} = \sqrt{\dfrac{9 + 16}{25}} = \sqrt{\dfrac{25}{25}} = \sqrt{1} = 1.$ A) 1 B) $\frac{7}{5}$ C) $\frac{12}{5}$ D) 5	32. A
33. Triangle ABC is half the area of the rectangle; but so is $\triangle ABE$. So the area of $\triangle ABE$ is 12. A) 18 B) 15 C) 12 D) 10	33. C
34. $4^5 \times 3^5 = 2^5 \times 2^5 \times 3^5 = (2^5 \times 3^5) \times 2^5 = (2 \times 3)^5 \times 2^5 = 6^5 \times 2^5.$ A) 2 B) 6^5 C) 1^5 D) 2^5	34. D
35. The lengths of the sides of the squares are 4 and 1. If we add both squares' perimeters together, we've counted the overlapping part twice, when it shouldn't be counted at all. Perimeter = 16 + 4 - 2 = 18. A) 18 B) 19 C) 20 D) 22	35. A
36. Since $2 \times 12 - 9 = \frac{1}{2} \times 12 + 9 = 15$, I am 12 years old. A) 99 years B) 18 years C) 12 years D) 9 years	36. C
37. Length of the 3rd side is between $11 - 9 = 2$ and $11 + 9 = 20$; perimeter is between $2 + 9 + 11 = 22$ and $20 + 9 + 11 = 40.$ A) 21 B) 23 C) 29 D) 31	37. B
38. In this product of *primes*, there's exactly one factor of 2 and and one of 5. The product is divisible by $2 \times 5 = 10$. A) 10 B) 100 C) 1000 D) 10^{1000}	38. A
39. If Lee's height is $3x$, then Pat, who is $\frac{1}{3}$ taller, has a height of $4x$. Thus, Lee's height is x less than Pat's or 25% less than $4x$. A) 20% B) 25% C) 30% D) $33\frac{1}{3}\%$	39. B
40. If each side is 1 unit thick, the inner dimensions of the refrigerator are $10 \times 8 \times 5$, and the refrigerator's inside volume is $10 \times 8 \times 5 = 400$ cubic units. A) 840 B) 700 C) 594 D) 400	40. D

The end of the contest ✍ **8**

Solutions

1990-91 Annual 8th Grade Contest
Tuesday, February 5, 1991

8

Contest Information

- **Solutions** Turn the page for detailed contest solutions (written in the question boxes) and letter answers (in the answer columns on the right).

- **Scores** When reviewing these questions, remember *this is a contest, not a test.* There is no "passing" or "failing" score. Few students score as high as 30 points (75% correct); students with even half that, 15 points, *deserve commendation!*

- **Answers & Rating Scale** Turn to page 163 for the letter answers to each question and the rating scale for this contest.

1.	$1990 + 1992 = 1990 + 1990 + 2 = 1991 + 1991$. A) 1991 B) 2×1991 C) 1991^2 D) 1994	1. B
2.	Of the 12 boys, one-fourth, or 3, were absent. Of the 15 girls, one-third, or 5, were absent. The total number absent was 8, so the total number present was $27 - 8 = 19$. A) 8 B) 19 C) 20 D) 21	2. B
3.	$0.33 + 0.033 + 0.0033 = 0.3663$. A) 0.3333 B) 0.3663 C) 0.6336 D) 0.6666	3. B
4.	The square of 4 is 16. The square root of 16 is 4. A) 4 B) 32 C) 64 D) 256	4. C
5.	$100 = 10 \times 10 = 10 \times (20 \times 0.5)$. A) 0.1 B) 0.2 C) 0.4 D) 0.5	5. D
6.	$99 - 0.99 = 99 - 1 + 0.01 = 98.01$. A) 0 B) 98 C) 98.01 D) 98.1	6. C
7.	$\sqrt{4+4+4+4} = \sqrt{16} = 4$. A) 2 B) 4 C) 8 D) 16	7. B
8.	The product includes 0 as a factor. A) −36 B) −6 C) 0 D) 36	8. C
9.	$10^4 - 1 = 10\,000 - 1 = 9\,999$. A) 9 B) 99 C) 999 D) 9999	9. D
10.	99.99 rounds to 100.0, so the answer is A. A) 100.0 B) 99.99 C) 99.9 D) 99.0	10. A
11.	$(-29) - (-30) + 1 = -29 + 30 + 1 = -29 + 31 = 2$. A) 0 B) 1 C) 2 D) 60	11. C
12.	They are all less than 1, but the closest to 1 is $\frac{99}{100}$. A) $\frac{7}{8}$ B) $\frac{4}{5}$ C) $\frac{9}{10}$ D) $\frac{99}{100}$	12. D
13.	$\sqrt{10201}$ is slightly more than 100 and ends in the digit 1. A) 100 B) 101 C) 102 D) 10201	13. B
14.	$\frac{1}{2} + \frac{1}{4} + \frac{1}{8} = \frac{4}{8} + \frac{2}{8} + \frac{1}{8} = \frac{7}{8}$. A) $\frac{3}{8}$ B) $\frac{5}{8}$ C) $\frac{7}{8}$ D) $\frac{9}{8}$	14. C
15.	The area of a right triangle is half the product of the legs. The area of this triangle is $(1/2)(20) = 10$. A) 10 B) 20 C) 40 D) 200	15. A

Go on to the next page ▶ **8**

16. $4^2 = 16 = 2^4$. A) 16 B) 8 C) 4 D) 2	16. C
17. In the diagram at the right, two parallel lines are intersected by a third line, forming a 75° angle as shown. Since $x = 75°$ and $y = 105°$, $x + y = 180°$. A) 75° B) 90° C) 105° D) 180°	17. D
18. $\dfrac{1 \times 4 \times 9 \times 16 \times 25}{\sqrt{1} \times \sqrt{4} \times \sqrt{9} \times \sqrt{16} \times \sqrt{25}} = \dfrac{1 \times 4 \times 9 \times 16 \times 25}{1 \times 2 \times 3 \times 4 \times 5} = 1 \times 2 \times 3 \times 4 \times 5$. A) 24 B) 120 C) 576 D) 1440	18. B
19. $25\% \times \frac{1}{2} \times 80 = \frac{1}{4} \times \frac{1}{2} \times \frac{80}{1} = \frac{80}{8} = 10$. A) 10 B) 20 C) 40 D) 80	19. A
20. The smallest angle cannot exceed the average (60°), so the sum of the other two is at least 180° – 60° = 120°. A) 119° B) 139° C) 159° D) 179°	20. A
21. There are 24 minutes between 1:55 A.M. and 2:19 A.M. Since 12 minutes is 1/5 of an hour, 24 minutes is 2/5 of an hour. A) $\frac{1}{5}$ B) $\frac{2}{5}$ C) $\frac{3}{5}$ D) $\frac{4}{5}$	21. B
22. 999×999 ends in the same digit as 9×9: the digit 1. A) 998001 B) 998003 C) 998007 D) 998009	22. A
23. Muffins usually cost 25¢ each. Today they are on sale for 20¢ each. Since \$5 normally buys 20 muffins, but today buys 25 muffins, Steve can buy 5 additional muffins during the sale. A) 2 B) 5 C) 6 D) 10	23. B
24. $(5 \times 30) \times (30 \times 5) = (5 \times 2 \times 15) \times (15 \times 2 \times 5) = 15^2 \times 2^2 \times 5^2$. A) 2×5 B) $2^2 \times 5$ C) 2×5^2 D) $2^2 \times 5^2$	24. D
25. $25\% = 1/4$, and 1/4 of 2 is 1/2, which is the reciprocal of 2, so the answer is 2. A) $\frac{1}{4}$ B) $\frac{1}{2}$ C) 2 D) 4	25. C
26. $(-1)^1 + (-1)^2 + (-1)^3 + \ldots + (-1)^{1991} = -1 + 1 - 1 + \ldots -1 = -1$. A) –1 B) 0 C) 1 D) –1991	26. A
27. To multiply by 1000, move the decimal 3 places to the right. A) 1991 B) 199.1 C) 19.91 D) 0.0001991	27. B
28. Try circles with circumferences 8π and 2π. Their radii are 4 and 1 and the areas are 16π and π. The area ratio is 16 to 1. A) 2:1 B) 4:1 C) 8:1 D) 16:1	28. D
29. The number 12 is 1 1/2 times as large as 8. A) 8 B) 12 C) 15 D) 18	29. A

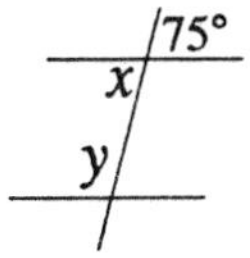

30. During the sale, it cost \$144 for a 1-year membership. But this represented a 50% savings from the regular price, so the regular price was twice as much, \$288. A) \$96 B) \$144 C) \$288 D) \$576	30. C
31. $\frac{10+1}{20+2} = \frac{11}{22} = \frac{10}{20} + 0.$ A) 0 B) $\frac{1}{2}$ C) 1 D) 2	31. A
32. In any triangle, the sum of the two smallest sides is greater than the third side, so 1,2,4 are not possible side-lengths. A) 1,2,4 B) 3,4,6 C) 4,5,7 D) 5,6,8	32. A
33. The product of any number of odd numbers is always odd. A) even B) odd C) prime D) negative	33. B
34. Ali lifts 3 times the weight that Keith lifts. If Ali lifts 40 kg more than Keith, Keith lifts 20 kg and Ali lifts 60 kg. A) 20 kg B) 40 kg C) 60 kg D) 120 kg	34. C
35. When $2\times2\times2\times2\times2\times2\times5\times5\times5\times5\times5$ is simplified, the product is $2\times10\times10\times10\times10\times10 = 200\,000$. A) 2 B) 5 C) 6 D) 11	35. B
36. The sum of the digits of 700 is 7. Adding 300 will make the new number 1000. The sum of the digits of the number 1000 is 1. No smaller sum is possible. A) 1 B) 8 C) 10 D) 307	36. A
37. The area of the circle is $\pi(5^2) = 25\pi$. The right triangle has a base of 10. Its altitude is a radius whose length is 5. The shaded region is $25\pi - 25$. A) $25\pi - 25$ B) $25\pi - 50$ C) $100\pi - 25$ D) $100\pi - 50$	37. A
38. The sum of two consecutive whole numbers is the sum of an even and an odd number, so the sum is odd. A) 1066 B) 1492 C) 1990 D) 1991	38. D
39. Let the nail polish cost 5 units and the lipstick cost 3 units. Then 15 bottles of nail polish cost 75 units, which is the same as the cost of 25 sticks of lipstick. A) 5 B) 9 C) 15 D) 25	39. D
40. If x people can do a job in d days, then 1 person would take xd days to finish and y people would finish in $\frac{xd}{y}$ days. A) $\frac{x}{yd}$ B) $\frac{xd}{y}$ C) $\frac{y}{xd}$ D) $\frac{yd}{x}$	40. B

The end of the contest 🖎 **8**

Answers & Ratings

ANSWERS 1982-83 7TH GRADE CONTEST

1. D	9. C	17. B	25. D	33. C
2. B	10. B	18. B	26. B	34. C
3. D	11. D	19. A	27. A	35. B
4. C	12. A	20. A	28. D	36. C
5. B	13. B	21. A	29. D	37. B
6. C	14. D	22. C	30. C	38. B
7. A	15. B	23. D	31. B	39. D
8. C	16. A	24. B	32. D	40. C

RATE YOURSELF!!!
for the 1982-83 7TH GRADE CONTEST

Score	Rating
37-40	Another Einstein
34-36	Mathematical Wizard
31-33	School Champion
27-30	Grade Level Champion
24-26	Best In The Class
21-23	Excellent Student
19-20	Good Student
16-18	Average Student
0-15	Better Luck Next Time

ANSWERS 1983-84 7TH GRADE CONTEST

1. A	9. A	17. D	25. B	33. A
2. D	10. D	18. D	26. C	34. D
3. C	11. B	19. D	27. D	35. D
4. D	12. D	20. A	28. C	36. D
5. A	13. B	21. D	29. D	37. C
6. C	14. D	22. D	30. C	38. C
7. D	15. B	23. D	31. C	39. C
8. B	16. C	24. D	32. B	40. B

RATE YOURSELF!!!
for the 1983-84 7th GRADE CONTEST

Score	Rating
35-40	Another Einstein
32-34	Mathematical Wizard
29-31	School Champion
25-28	Grade Level Champion
22-24	Best In The Class
19-21	Excellent Student
17-18	Good Student
14-16	Average Student
0-13	Better Luck Next Time

ANSWERS 1984-85 7TH GRADE CONTEST

1. B	9. A	17. B	25. C	33. D
2. B	10. D	18. D	26. A	34. A
3. C	11. C	19. A	27. B	35. B
4. B	12. D	20. B	28. D	36. C
5. A	13. C	21. C	29. D	37. A
6. D	14. B	22. A	30. B	38. C
7. C	15. A	23. B	31. C	39. D
8. C	16. B	24. B	32. B	40. D

RATE YOURSELF!!!
for the 1984-85 7TH GRADE CONTEST

Score	Rating
37-40	Another Einstein
34-36	Mathematical Wizard
31-33	School Champion
28-30	Grade Level Champion
24-27	Best In The Class
21-23	Excellent Student
18-20	Good Student
15-17	Average Student
0-14	Better Luck Next Time

ANSWERS 1985-86 7TH GRADE CONTEST

1. A	9. C	17. D	25. D	33. B
2. D	10. D	18. A	26. C	34. D
3. A	11. B	19. A	27. D	35. C
4. B	12. B	20. C	28. C	36. B
5. C	13. A	21. D	29. A	37. A
6. D	14. B	22. A	30. C	38. C
7. C	15. A	23. C	31. C	39. A
8. B	16. D	24. B	32. C	40. C

RATE YOURSELF!!!
for the 1985-86 7TH GRADE CONTEST

Score	Rating
37-40	Another Einstein
34-36	Mathematical Wizard
31-33	School Champion
29-30	Grade Level Champion
26-28	Best In The Class
23-25	Excellent Student
20-22	Good Student
16-19	Average Student
0-15	Better Luck Next Time

ANSWERS 1986-87 7TH GRADE CONTEST

1. A	9. C	17. C	25. C	33. D
2. A	10. A	18. A	26. A	34. C
3. D	11. D	19. C	27. B	35. B
4. B	12. C	20. C	28. B	36. D
5. B	13. A	21. B	29. B	37. A
6. D	14. B	22. D	30. B	38. C
7. A	15. A	23. D	31. C	39. C
8. D	16. B	24. C	32. A	40. D

RATE YOURSELF!!!
for the 1986-87 7TH GRADE CONTEST

Score		Rating
36-40		Another Einstein
33-35		Mathematical Wizard
31-32		School Champion
28-30		Grade Level Champion
24-27		Best In The Class
22-23		Excellent Student
18-21		Good Student
14-17		Average Student
0-13		Better Luck Next Time

ANSWERS 1987-88 7TH GRADE CONTEST

1. B	9. C	17. D	25. D	33. D
2. C	10. C	18. B	26. B	34. B
3. D	11. A	19. C	27. A	35. B
4. C	12. A	20. A	28. D	36. D
5. B	13. D	21. C	29. B	37. C
6. B	14. B	22. D	30. A	38. B
7. A	15. C	23. B	31. C	39. A
8. D	16. A	24. D	32. D	40. C

RATE YOURSELF!!!
for the 1987-88 7TH GRADE CONTEST

Score	Rating
36-40	Another Einstein
33-35	Mathematical Wizard
30-32	School Champion
27-29	Grade Level Champion
24-26	Best In The Class
21-23	Excellent Student
19-20	Good Student
15-18	Average Student
0-14	Better Luck Next Time

ANSWERS 1988-89 7TH GRADE CONTEST

1. D	9. B	17. D	25. A	33. A
2. A	10. C	18. C	26. D	34. B
3. D	11. C	19. B	27. C	35. D
4. B	12. C	20. B	28. C	36. C
5. C	13. A	21. C	29. C	37. C
6. B	14. B	22. A	30. B	38. B
7. B	15. A	23. A	31. D	39. A
8. C	16. A	24. A	32. D	40. C

RATE YOURSELF!!!
for the 1988-89 7TH GRADE CONTEST

Score	Rating
35-40	Another Einstein
32-34	Mathematical Wizard
30-31	School Champion
28-29	Grade Level Champion
26-27	Best In The Class
22-25	Excellent Student
19-21	Good Student
15-18	Average Student
0-14	Better Luck Next Time

ANSWERS 1989-90 7TH GRADE CONTEST

1. D	9. B	17. B	25. D	33. D
2. B	10. D	18. A	26. B	34. C
3. C	11. C	19. D	27. D	35. A
4. A	12. A	20. A	28. C	36. A
5. D	13. A	21. A	29. C	37. B
6. D	14. D	22. B	30. B	38. C
7. B	15. A	23. D	31. C	39. B
8. A	16. C	24. C	32. A	40. C

RATE YOURSELF!!!
for the 1989-90 7TH GRADE CONTEST

Score	Rating
36-40	Another Einstein
33-35	Mathematical Wizard
31-32	School Champion
28-30	Grade Level Champion
25-27	Best In The Class
23-24	Excellent Student
19-22	Good Student
15-18	Average Student
0-14	Better Luck Next Time

ANSWERS 1990-91 7TH GRADE CONTEST

1. B	9. B	17. A	25. B	33. A
2. D	10. C	18. A	26. D	34. C
3. B	11. D	19. B	27. D	35. B
4. C	12. B	20. C	28. C	36. D
5. A	13. A	21. C	29. A	37. D
6. B	14. C	22. C	30. D	38. C
7. D	15. D	23. D	31. C	39. C
8. B	16. B	24. A	32. A	40. C

RATE YOURSELF!!!
for the 1990-91 7TH GRADE CONTEST

Score	Rating
38-40	Another Einstein
35-37	Mathematical Wizard
33-34	School Champion
29-32	Grade Level Champion
27-28	Best In The Class
24-26	Excellent Student
21-23	Good Student
18-20	Average Student
0-17	Better Luck Next Time

ANSWERS 1982-83 8TH GRADE CONTEST

1. D	9. D	17. B	25. D	33. C
2. D	10. D	18. A	26. D	34. C
3. A	11. B	19. A	27. C	35. B
4. C	12. B	20. A	28. B	36. D
5. C	13. D	21. A	29. D	37. D
6. C	14. B	22. B	30. A	38. B
7. D	15. A	23. D	31. C	39. C
8. A	16. D	24. B	32. A	40. B

RATE YOURSELF!!!
for the 1982-83 8TH GRADE CONTEST

Score	Rating
36-40	Another Einstein
33-35	Mathematical Wizard
30-32	School Champion
27-29	Grade Level Champion
24-26	Best In The Class
21-23	Excellent Student
18-20	Good Student
15-17	Average Student
0-14	Better Luck Next Time

ANSWERS 1983-84 8TH GRADE CONTEST

1. D	9. B	17. B	25. D	33. D
2. C	10. C	18. C	26. D	34. B
3. A	11. A	19. D	27. C	35. C
4. D	12. D	20. D	28. A	36. D
5. D	13. C	21. B	29. C	37. C
6. D	14. D	22. C	30. D	38. C
7. D	15. D	23. B	31. D	39. B
8. D	16. D	24. D	32. D	40. C

RATE YOURSELF!!!
for the 1983-84 8TH GRADE CONTEST

Score	Rating
36-40	Another Einstein
33-35	Mathematical Wizard
30-32	School Champion
27-29	Grade Level Champion
24-26	Best In The Class
21-23	Excellent Student
18-20	Good Student
16-17	Average Student
0-15	Better Luck Next Time

ANSWERS 1984-85 8TH GRADE CONTEST

1. D	9. A	17. B	25. D	33. C
2. B	10. B	18. B	26. B	34. C
3. B	11. A	19. A	27. A	35. C
4. C	12. D	20. D	28. C	36. C
5. C	13. D	21. B	29. D	37. B
6. C	14. C	22. C	30. B	38. D
7. A	15. A	23. B	31. A	39. D
8. C	16. D	24. C	32. A	40. C

RATE YOURSELF!!!
for the 1984-85 8TH GRADE CONTEST

Score	Rating
38-40	Another Einstein
34-37	Mathematical Wizard
31-33	School Champion
28-30	Grade Level Champion
25-27	Best In The Class
22-24	Excellent Student
18-21	Good Student
15-17	Average Student
0-14	Better Luck Next Time

ANSWERS 1985-86 8TH GRADE CONTEST

1. D	9. D	17. D	25. C	33. A
2. A	10. A	18. B	26. C	34. B
3. B	11. A	19. B	27. A	35. D
4. C	12. A	20. A	28. D	36. D
5. C	13. C	21. A	29. C	37. C
6. A	14. C	22. D	30. B	38. C
7. B	15. D	23. D	31. B	39. D
8. A	16. C	24. C	32. C	40. D

RATE YOURSELF!!!

for the 1985-86 8TH GRADE CONTEST

Score		Rating
37-40		Another Einstein
33-36		Mathematical Wizard
30-32		School Champion
27-29		Grade Level Champion
24-26		Best In The Class
21-23		Excellent Student
18-20		Good Student
16-17		Average Student
0-15		Better Luck Next Time

ANSWERS 1986-87 8TH GRADE CONTEST

1. A	9. A	17. A	25. C	33. B
2. C	10. A	18. C	26. D	34. D
3. D	11. C	19. B	27. A	35. C
4. A	12. C	20. C	28. C	36. C
5. D	13. B	21. B	29. B	37. D
6. B	14. D	22. C	30. B	38. D
7. D	15. C	23. A	31. D	39. B
8. B	16. D	24. A	32. A	40. A

RATE YOURSELF!!!
for the 1986-87 8TH GRADE CONTEST

Score	Rating
37-40	Another Einstein
34-36	Mathematical Wizard
32-33	School Champion
29-31	Grade Level Champion
26-28	Best In The Class
23-25	Excellent Student
20-22	Good Student
17-19	Average Student
0-16	Better Luck Next Time

ANSWERS 1987-88 8TH GRADE CONTEST

1. C	9. C	17. A	25. D	33. B
2. A	10. B	18. C	26. A	34. A
3. B	11. D	19. B	27. A	35. C
4. C	12. B	20. C	28. D	36. D
5. A	13. D	21. C	29. A	37. B
6. A	14. D	22. A	30. D	38. A
7. D	15. C	23. C	31. B	39. B
8. B	16. B	24. B	32. C	40. C

RATE YOURSELF!!!
for the 1987-88 8TH GRADE CONTEST

Score		Rating
38-40		Another Einstein
35-37		Mathematical Wizard
32-34		School Champion
29-31		Grade Level Champion
26-28		Best In The Class
24-25		Excellent Student
21-23		Good Student
18-20		Average Student
0-17		Better Luck Next Time

ANSWERS 1988-89 8TH GRADE CONTEST

1. C	9. D	17. D	25. D	33. A
2. C	10. B	18. A	26. C	34. B
3. B	11. B	19. B	27. C	35. B
4. B	12. D	20. A	28. A	36. B
5. B	13. D	21. B	29. D	37. D
6. C	14. C	22. D	30. A	38. C
7. A	15. A	23. C	31. D	39. C
8. A	16. B	24. C	32. B	40. D

RATE YOURSELF!!!
for the 1988-89 8TH GRADE CONTEST

Score	Rating
37-40	Another Einstein
34-36	Mathematical Wizard
31-33	School Champion
28-30	Grade Level Champion
25-27	Best In The Class
22-24	Excellent Student
19-21	Good Student
16-18	Average Student
0-15	Better Luck Next Time

ANSWERS 1989-90 8TH GRADE CONTEST

1. B	9. B	17. B	25. B	33. C
2. D	10. D	18. C	26. C	34. D
3. B	11. B	19. D	27. A	35. A
4. D	12. A	20. C	28. C	36. C
5. C	13. D	21. A	29. B	37. B
6. D	14. A	22. B	30. A	38. A
7. C	15. C	23. B	31. B	39. B
8. C	16. A	24. D	32. A	40. D

RATE YOURSELF!!!
for the 1989-90 8TH GRADE CONTEST

Score		Rating
37-40		Another Einstein
34-36		Mathematical Wizard
32-33		School Champion
29-31		Grade Level Champion
26-28		Best In The Class
23-25		Excellent Student
20-22		Good Student
17-19		Average Student
0-16		Better Luck Next Time

ANSWERS 1990-91 8TH GRADE CONTEST

1. B	9. D	17. D	25. C	33. B
2. B	10. A	18. B	26. A	34. C
3. B	11. C	19. A	27. B	35. B
4. C	12. D	20. A	28. D	36. A
5. D	13. B	21. B	29. A	37. A
6. C	14. C	22. A	30. C	38. D
7. B	15. A	23. B	31. A	39. D
8. C	16. C	24. D	32. A	40. B

RATE YOURSELF!!!
for the 1990-91 8TH GRADE CONTEST

Score	Rating
37-40	Another Einstein
33-36	Mathematical Wizard
30-32	School Champion
27-29	Grade Level Champion
25-26	Best In The Class
23-24	Excellent Student
20-22	Good Student
17-19	Average Student
0-16	Better Luck Next Time

Math League Contest Books
4th Grade Through High School Levels

Written by Steven R. Conrad and Daniel Flegler, recipients of President Reagan's 1985 Presidential Awards for Excellence in Mathematics Teaching, each book provides schools and students with:

- Contests designed for a 30-minute period
- Problems ranging from straightforward to challenging
- Contests from 4th grade through high school
- Easy-to-use format

1-10 copies of any one book: $12.95 each ($16.95 Canadian)
11 or more copies of any one book: $9.95 each ($12.95 Canadian)

Use the form below (or a copy) to order your books

Name:_____

Address:_____

City:_____State:_____Zip:_____

Available Titles	# of Copies	Cost
Math Contests—Grades 4, 5, 6 (Vol. 1) Contests from 1979-80 through 1985-86	_____	_____
Math Contests—Grades 4, 5, 6 (Vol. 2) Contests from 1986-87 through 1990-91	_____	_____
Math Contests—Grades 7 & 8 (Vol. 1) Contests from 1977-78 through 1981-82	_____	_____
Math Contests—Grades 7 & 8 (Vol. 2) Contests from 1982-83 through 1990-91	_____	_____
Math Contests—High School (Vol. 1) Contests from 1977-78 through 1981-82	_____	_____
Math Contests—High School (Vol. 2) Contests from 1982-83 through 1990-91	_____	_____
Shipping and Handling		$3.00

Please allow 4-6 weeks for delivery   Total: $_____

☐ Check or Purchase Order Enclosed; *or*
☐ Visa / MasterCard # _____
☐ Exp. Date _____   Signature _____

Mail your order with payment to:

Math League Press
P.O. Box 720
Tenafly, NJ 07670

Phone: (201) 568-6328 • Fax: (201) 816-0125